AERIAL
COMBAT
The World's Great Air Battles

AERIAL COMBAT
The World's Great Air Battles

Robert Jackson

Foreword by Alan Clark

Galahad Books New York City

Library of Congress Catalog Card Number: 76-9453
ISBN 0-88365-361-3

Filmset and printed Offset Litho in Great Britain by
Cox & Wyman Ltd, London, Fakenham and Reading
Published by arrangement with Weidenfeld and Nicolson,
London, England.

CONTENTS

Foreword

by Alan Clark

What is it about aerial combat that endows it with a particular romance and fascination? Surely, and above all else, it is the personal identity, the direct pitting of individual qualities – courage, judgement, keenness of vision and reflex, and the ability to control machinery of immense complication and power.

For over three centuries, or even longer, from the time of the discovery of gunpowder until the invention of the aeroplane the practice of warfare, and combat itself, sank ever lower into anonymity. The Big Battalions decided the issue. And as the use of explosives widened so did the range at which these encounters took place lengthen, and the private bravery and accomplishment at arms of the participants diminish in importance. Of course, there were savage struggles, hand-to-hand, at Blenheim, at Waterloo, at Gettysburg, but the essential determinants were the deployment of firepower and mass. At Verdun tens of thousands of soldiers lost their lives crawling backwards and forwards through storms of high explosive remotely directed upon them by artillery-men whom they never saw, nor could ever hope to reach with their weapons.

But aerial combat was from the very outset – and remains even to this day – exclusively individualist, and the proliferation of high technology accentuates the importance of the human brain in interpreting its messages, as it does the virtues of bravery and calculating risk. There is a direct qualitative link between the observer hammering desperately with gloved hand against the jamming magazine of his Lewis gun as the pursuing Fokker closes the range, and the pilot of an Israeli F4 diving to ground level as he attempts to shake off the pursuing SAM.

In aerial combat there is also a certain clinical detachment. The presence of your opponent is always felt. The intrusion of his willpower and cunning warp the contest, as they do over a chessboard. But his appearance, the many clues and inferences to a man's character, that can be drawn from a scrutiny of his face and eyes, remain a mystery. Nor can the victor ever see the actual affect of his prowess; those tenths of a second when a whiplash of bullets tear across his enemy's cockpit, smashing bone, leather and instruments; the sudden loss of pressurization as the canopy shatters at altitude, the deluge of Glycol, the orange blast of ignited fuel – even this last is observed only remotely, a minute gyrating speck signifying a transient personal triumph and a brief lightening of danger.

Airmen, then, are different from other soldiers. They have to be navigators, mathematicians, experts in meteorology and geography. They have to be marksmen and athletes. But without the killer instinct, the animal tenacity that holds the jaws clenched for those critical seconds longer than seems physically possible, their survival is at risk. In the gallery of warfare they are above all others, an élite, and their tales are the tales of heroes.

1 The First Air Battles

At 6.25 on the morning of 13 August 1914 a flimsy B.E.2a biplane took off from a grass field near Dover and pointed its nose out over the English Channel, towards France. Flown by Lieutenant H. D. Harvey-Kelly, it was followed by forty more machines; B.E.2s, Blériots, Henri Farmans, B.E.8s and Avro 504s.

By noon all but one – forced down with engine trouble – had arrived at Amiens, to be received enthusiastically by the French population. The First World War was ten days old, and the Royal Flying Corps had arrived in France.

On the outbreak of war the fledgeling Royal Flying Corps – formed a little over two years earlier, in April 1912 – possessed a grand total of 180 aircraft, and by dawn on 14 August sixty-four of them had been sent to France to equip the four squadrons that were to fly in support of the British Expeditionary Force. Their task was reconnaissance; the machines they flew were unarmed – except for the small-arms carried by pilots and observers – and no one had yet seriously considered the aircraft as an offensive weapon. In the eyes of most senior British Army officers its function was to supplement the cavalry in the observation role, and most regarded with scepticism the idea that the aeroplane could ever be more than an interesting novelty. Others, however, were far-sighted enough to recognize the aircraft's military potential – and even as the RFC units in France were preparing to carry out their first missions, a certain Lieutenant-Colonel Hugh Trenchard was setting about the task of organizing the squadrons that remained in England into an efficient force that would be capable of supporting British land operations on the Continent to the full.

On 16 August Nos. 2, 3 and 4 Squadrons left Amiens for Maubeuge, and the next morning Captain Joubert de la Ferté in a No. 3 Squadron Blériot and Lieutenant G. W. Mapplebeck flying a B.E.2a of No. 4 Squadron took off to carry out the RFC's first air reconnaissance of the war. Joubert was to reconnoitre the area around Genappe and Mapplebeck was to search for enemy cavalry reportedly at Gembloux. The latter pilot completed his mission successfully, but Joubert got lost in cloud and finally landed at Tournai, where he got his bearings before returning to Maubeuge.

More reconnaissance flights were made during the next few days, and on 22 August the RFC sustained its first casualty when an observer, Sergeant-Major Jillings, was wounded in the leg by a rifle bullet over Maffle. Twelve flights were made over the Brussels area, and one of these – made by Captain L. E. O. Charlton and Lieutenant V. H. N. Wadham of No. 3 Squadron – had important results. Landing at Moerbeke to inquire about German troop movements, they were informed that large numbers of the enemy were passing through Grammont, two miles away. Charlton and Wadham took off and flew in that direction, and soon sighted a long column of German troops and cavalry moving westwards along the Brussels–Ninove

ABOVE The Henri Farman HF 20, used in action from the first day of the First World War for reconnaissance.

road. It was Field-Marshal von Kluck's II Corps, attempting to outflank and encircle the Belgian Army – which, thanks to the timely information brought back by the two airmen, was able to extricate itself from the trap. On that same day Lieutenants V. Waterfall and C. G. G. Bayly of No. 5 Squadron were shot down behind the enemy lines; both managed to get away, but the wreckage of their Avro 504 gave the Germans their first indication that the British Army was about to go into action against them.

On 23 August the Battle of Mons raged, and that morning the RFC HQ was pulled back to Le Cateau. The British pilots were extremely active throughout the days that followed but were badly hampered by the constantly changing location of their HQ as the retreat from Mons developed. Nevertheless they managed to keep a watch on all enemy troop movements, enabling the Allied commanders to build up a highly accurate picture of the course of events. On 4 September, air reconnaissance showed that von Kluck's forces had marched directly into a pocket between the Fifth and Sixth French Armies. Less than twenty-four hours later the position was extremely favourable for a general Allied counter-offensive – the great onslaught known as the Battle of the Marne, one of the turning-points of the First World War. During the battle Nos. 5 and 3 Squadrons were attached to the British First and Second Armies, commanded by Field-Marshals Sir Douglas Haig and Sir Horace Smith-Dorrien, and the aircraft came under the direct control of the various Army Corps commanders. In a despatch of 7 September the BEF Commander – Sir John French – commended the

RFC for its valiant efforts during this decisive period. 'Their skill, energy and perseverance', he wrote, 'have been beyond all praise. They have furnished me with the most complete and accurate information which has been of incalculable value in the conduct of operations.'

ABOVE The B.E.2c, one of the first British aircraft to reach France at the outbreak of war and widely used for reconnaissance and light bombing until May 1917.

By this time aircraft of the RFC and the German Flying Corps were beginning to meet one another fairly frequently over the battle front. As yet none of the aircraft of either side was armed as a matter of routine, although their crews carried side-arms and often carbines. The crews of No. 5 Squadron had been experimenting with the mounting of a machine-gun in the observers' cockpits of their Henri Farmans, but the extra weight resulted in an enormous sacrifice in performance. The Farmans were among six RFC machines that chased a German observation aircraft over Maubeuge on 22 August, but the enemy had the advantage of height and got away. Then, on the twenty-fifth, three B.E.2as of No. 2 Squadron trapped an enemy aircraft and flew round and round it, taking pot-shots with carbines until the German made a forced landing. The crew escaped into a wood, and their aircraft was set on fire by the pilot of a B.E. who landed alongside it. A second German aircraft and its crew were captured later that day near Le Quesnoy.

During September the weather was the RFC's main enemy; violent rainstorms lashed across the countryside, destroying several aircraft, and by the twelfth only ten machines were serviceable. Ground crews worked day and night to patch up the remainder, for the Battle of the Aisne was developing and every available machine was needed. During this battle the RFC

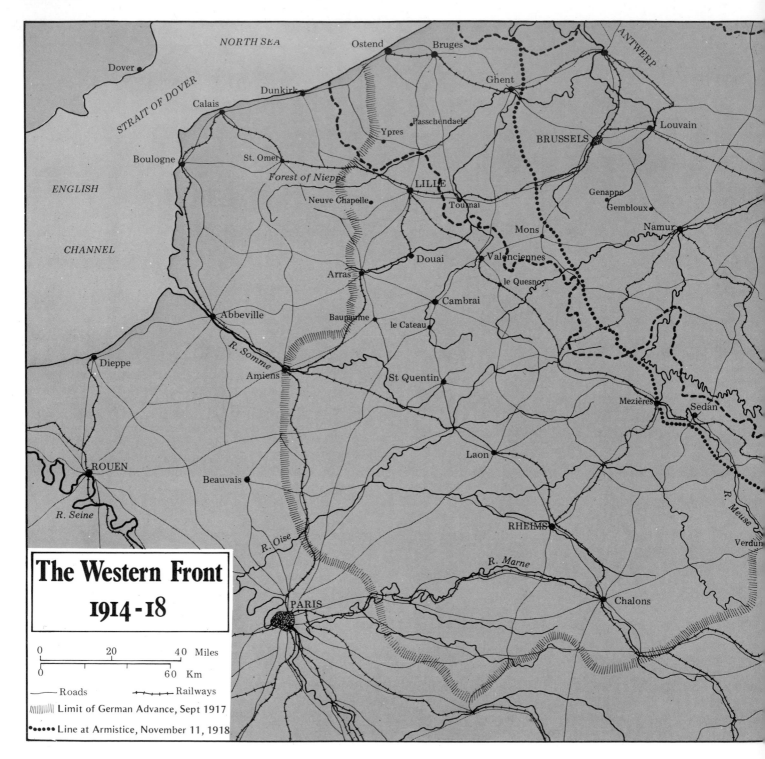

The Western Front
1914-18

```
0          20          40  Miles
0                  60  Km
```

—— Roads   +++++ Railways

|||||||| Limit of German Advance, Sept 1917

•••••• Line at Armistice, November 11, 1918

employed several new techniques, including the use of wireless telegraphy to direct artillery shoots, and on several occasions grenades and steel darts – the latter a French invention – wcrc dropped on enemy troops. The Battle of the Aisne gave way to the bloody First Battle of Ypres in October, but the RFC – with its HQ now at St Omer – was again handicapped by appalling weather, although whenever possible reconnaissances were carried out up to twenty miles behind the enemy lines. There were occasional encounters between British and German aircraft, culminating in a fight on 22 November

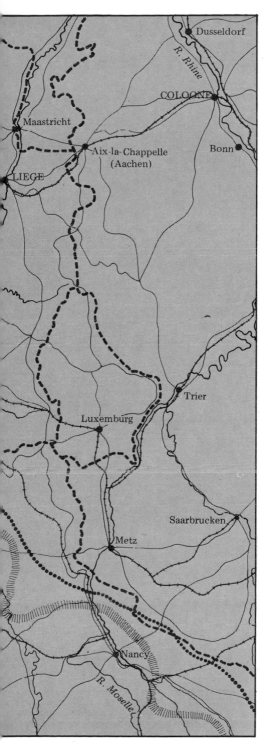

between an Albatros and an Avro 504 fitted with a Lewis gun in the observer's cockpit. The observer, Lieutenant L. G. Small, emptied two drums in the direction of the German machine, which went down to make a forced landing. The two-man crew was captured.

By this time reinforcements had arrived in the shape of No. 6 Squadron, which – equipped with B.E.8s and Henri Farmans – carried out local reconnaissance work from Bailleul in support of IV Corps from 8 October. Its first casualties were suffered on 27 October, when Lieutenants Rawson-Shaw and Mayne ran out of petrol behind the German lines, having encountered gale-force winds, and were taken prisoner. A few days later Captain Marsh forced down a Fokker intact near St Omer.

Early in 1915 a considerable step forward was taken in the science of air fighting when the French developed a device that enabled a machine-gun to fire forwards through the propeller blades of the aircraft on which it was mounted. The device – which was extremely simple, although somewhat dangerous – consisted of triangular steel wedges, fitted to the near side of each propeller blade so that any bullets that struck it would be deflected. It was tested in action by Roland Garros, who had already achieved fame as one of France's pioneer aviators before the war; he shot down six enemy aircraft in three weeks before being forced down with engine trouble and taken prisoner.

Garros's aircraft – a Morane – was immediately flown to Berlin for examination. One of the engineers summoned to look it over was Anthony

RIGHT An early attempt at mounting a gun on a French aircraft.

Fokker – a young Dutchman who had been designing military aircraft for Germany since 1913. Fearing that the Allies would soon have hundreds of aircraft equipped with forward-firing guns, the German High Command gave Fokker just forty-eight hours to design a comparable method of shooting through a whirling propeller disc.

Fokker immediately plunged into his task. He realized straight away that Garros's method was too primitive and dangerous: the force of the bullets striking the deflector plates would sooner or later shatter the propeller and shake the engine from its mounting. What was needed, Fokker reasoned, was some method whereby the propeller itself was geared to fire the machine-gun – a synchronizing device so that every bullet passed between the revolving blades. He fitted a small knob to the propeller which struck a cam when it revolved; the cam was attached by a wire to the hammer of the gun. He tested the device – and it worked. After a few refinements, he was ready to demonstrate the technique to the General Staff. They were suitably impressed, and gave orders for Fokker's invention to be tested operationally at the front.

Meanwhile, in April 1915, Nos. 7 and 8 Squadrons of the RFC had arrived in France, and had immediately been sent into action in support of the hard-pressed British ground forces at Ypres, the scene of the first German gas

TOP The famous Fokker E.I fighter fitted with a Spandau machine-gun on top of the fuselage fired with the Fokker interrupter device.

ABOVE The brilliant young Dutch aircraft designer, Anthony Fokker.

OPPOSITE Shot down by German planes, a Farman falls burning to the ground.

attack. No. 2 Squadron also took part in these operations, and during one attack on 26 April one of its pilots, 2nd Lieutenant W. B. Rhodes-Moorehouse, was mortally wounded while bombing the railway line west of Courtrai from 300 feet through intense anti-aircraft fire. He was posthumously awarded the Victoria Cross, the first of nineteen to be won by the RFC and RNAS before November 1918.

The battles of Neuve Chapelle and Ypres vindicated the RFC in the eyes of the British field commanders, including those who had been contemptuous of the use of aircraft for military purposes, and by early May air reconnaissance was held to be of such value that some vital ground operations were postponed because aircraft were not immediately available. Co-operation between aircraft and artillery reached a new level of efficiency with the use of W/T and revised methods of air-ground signalling – a vital step, because at this stage in the war shells were in short supply and there was no margin for unnecessary wastage.

The new techniques were put into practice during a series of actions that took place during the summer of 1915, the most important of which was a highly successful attack by the 6th Division at Hooge on 9 August, and culminated in the Battle of Loos. It was here that the RFC, commanded by Trenchard since 19 August, played its biggest part so far. During the first three weeks of September the squadrons of the First Wing worked over the enemy lines from dawn to dusk, bringing back hundreds of photographs and transmitting visual observations to forty wireless posts on the ground. When the First Army's bombardment opened on 21 September, the Second and Third Wings launched an all-out bombing attack with thirty-four aircraft against the Lille-Douai-Valenciennes railway triangle. The preliminary attack on the twenty-third achieved several rail cuts and a direct hit on a goods-train, and on the twenty-sixth the RFC's bombs hit two ammunition trains at Valenciennes. Twenty truckloads of shells exploded, putting the junction out of action for several days at a crucial point of the battle. The bombing attacks went on for six days, during which period the RFC dropped five and a half tons of bombs for the loss of two aircraft, destroying or

damaging five trains and hitting a total of fifteen targets up to thirty-six miles behind the enemy lines.

By 25 September 1915 there were twelve RFC squadrons in France. One of them, No. 11, was equipped with the Vickers F.B.5 'Gunbus' pusher biplane, armed with a Lewis gun firing from the forward cockpit, and was the first squadron formed specifically for air fighting. By the time it arrived in France in July 1915 combats between British and German aircraft were a frequent occurrence, but the standard air armament was still the rifle. As the importance of air reconnaissance increased, however, so did the importance of preventing the other side's aircraft from carrying it out, and from that moment the steady evolution of the fighter aircraft was assured. The first Vickers F.B.5s were received by No. 5 Squadron early in 1915, and on 10 May one of them shot down a German aircraft near Lille. Air combats intensified during the summer months, and one of them resulted in the award of the RFC's second Victoria Cross. It happened in the evening of 25 July 1915, when Captain L. G. Hawker, patrolling the front line in a Bristol Scout of No. 6 Squadron, attacked a German aircraft over Passchendaele. The enemy escaped by diving; so did a second, which Hawker attacked a few minutes later over Houthulst Forest. Hawker then climbed to 11,000 feet and sighted a third enemy aircraft over Hooge. Closing to within a hundred yards he opened fire with his Lewis gun; the German aircraft burst into flames and crashed near Zonnebeke.

It was in July 1915 that Anthony Fokker's invention began to make its impact felt on the Western Front with the service debut of his E.I monoplane, armed with a Spandau machine-gun firing through the propeller disc. This was a development that still eluded the Allies, whose only aircraft fitted with forward-firing machine-guns were slow 'pusher' types. A few weeks later the German Flying Corps began to receive an improved model, the Fokker E.III, so beginning a martyrdom of the RFC and the French Air Corps that was to last for a year. The German fighter pilots now held all the cards; cruising at altitude, they could select their target at leisure and make a diving attack on it, using their whole aircraft as an aiming platform, and since their machine-guns were belt-fed (as opposed to the drum-fed weapons used by the majority of British and French types), they were able to carry more ammunition and consequently deliver longer bursts of fire. The B.E.2s suffered particularly heavy losses at the hands of the Fokkers, for the B.E. had a vulnerable blind spot under its belly and the German pilots exploited

ABOVE Captain L. G. Hawker, the winner of the RFC's second Victoria Cross.

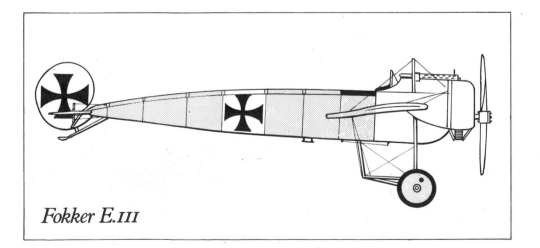

Fokker E.III

RIGHT Oswald Boelcke, one of the
first German aces.

FAR RIGHT A German propaganda
postcard commemorating another
ace, Max Immelmann.

BELOW The wreckage of
Immelmann's plane which crashed
under mysterious circumstances on
18 June 1916.

this to the full, zooming up under their victims and firing as they went. The B.E.s' observers could only retaliate when the Fokkers climbed up into view, by which time it was usually too late. The autumn of 1915 marked the ascendancy of the first German aces, Max Immelmann and Oswald Boelcke, whose scores mounted steadily towards the end of the year. Immelmann himself graphically described his fifth victory, a B.E.2c, his words emphasizing the hopelessness of the British aircraft's position:

I took off at 9.30 am on October 26th. I had just climbed to 3500 when I saw an enemy airman fly over the lines by Arras and make for Cambrai. I let him fly on eastward for a while. Then I took up the pursuit, hiding behind his tail all the time. I followed him for about a quarter of an hour in this fashion. My fingers were itching to shoot, but I controlled myself and withheld my fire until I was within sixty metres of him.

Knack-knack-knack . . . went my gun. Fifty rounds, and then a long flame shot out of his engine. Another fifty rounds at the pilot. Now his fate was sealed. He went down in wide spirals to land. Almost every bullet of my first series went home. Elevator, rudder, wings, engine, tank and control wires were shot up. The pilot [Captain C. Dalgy] had a bullet in the right upper arm. I had also shot his right thumb away. The machine had received forty hits. The observer [Lieutenant R. J. Slade] was unwounded. His machine-gun was in perfect working order but he had not fired a single shot, so complete was the surprise I had sprung on him. (Franz Immelmann, *Immelmann, the Eagle of Lille*, John Hamilton Ltd., London 1931.)

The leading German air fighter of 1915 was Oswald Boelcke, who scored forty official victories between 6 July and 26 October 1916. Thirty-one of these were two-seaters. Boelcke was killed on 28 October 1916 in an air collision with one of his own pilots, Lieutenant Erwin Boehme; the latter went on to become one of Germany's leading fighter aces, scoring twenty-four victories before being shot down by Captain John A. Pattern of No. 10 Squadron RFC on 29 November 1917. Max Immelmann, who was credited with thirteen victories, crashed to his death on 18 June 1916 under somewhat mysterious circumstances; according to one version he was shot down by Corporal J. H. Waller, the observer of a No. 25 Squadron F.E.2b, but another theory is that his Fokker's synchronization gear failed to work properly and he shot off his own propeller, causing the engine to break away from its mountings and leading to the break-up of his whole aircraft.

2 Trial of Strength

The success of the 'Fokker Scourge' towards the end of 1915 led to a revision of the RFC's tactics. On 14 January 1916 General Trenchard issued the following order: 'Until the Royal Flying Corps is in possession of a machine as good, or better than, the German Fokker, it seems that a change in policy and tactics has become necessary. In order to ensure that reconnaissance and photography patrols are allowed a fair chance of success, all fighter aircraft will raid prominent enemy aerodromes and attack any hostile machine that offers combat.' He also directed that 'as a hard-and-fast rule . . . a machine proceeding on a reconnaissance must be escorted by at least three other fighting machines. These machines must fly in close formation and a reconnaissance should not be continued if any of the machines become detached. Flying in close formation must be practised by all pilots.'

During the weeks that followed the RFC crews tried out various battle formations, with mixed success. In a typical arrangement, the formation was led by the reconnaissance aircraft, with a close escort 500 feet above on either quarter and a third escort 1000 feet above and to the rear. These tactics sometimes worked; on 7 February 1916, for example, four British aircraft successfully fought off fourteen Fokkers, but more often than not the escorts themselves had to fight for their lives against greatly superior numbers and leave the unfortunate reconnaissance machine to fend for itself. Apart from that, the provision of escorts meant that fewer aircraft could be spared for Army co-operation work – a serious disadvantage in 1916, with the Allies planning a series of major offensives.

The only real solution was to introduce fighter aircraft that were at least a match for the Fokkers, machines that could maintain constant patrols over the front and challenge the German aircraft in combat whenever they appeared. The tragic fact was that Britain had possessed such an aircraft – the F.E.2 – since 1913, but it had been a year before the first twelve were ordered from the Royal Aircraft Factory, and it was May 1915 before the first few production examples arrived in France for service with No. 6 Squadron. A two-seat 'pusher' type powered by a 120-hp Beardmore engine and armed with one Lewis gun in the front cockpit and a second on a telescopic mounting firing upwards over the wing centre-section, the F.E.2b was slightly slower than the Fokker E.III but a match in manœuvrability.

The first RFC squadron to be entirely equipped with the F.E.2b was No. 20, which arrived in France on 23 January 1916. It was followed, on 8 February, by No. 24 Squadron, equipped with D.H.2s. The D.H.2 was a single-seat 'pusher' type powered by a 100-hp Monosoupape and mounting a single Lewis gun installed on a pivot at the port side of the cockpit. The prototype had been sent to France in July 1915 for trials with No. 5 Squadron, but had been shot down over enemy territory a month later. Rugged and highly manœuvrable, the D.H.2 was to achieve more success in action against the Fokkers than any other Allied fighter type.

No. 24 Squadron, commanded by Major Hawker, VC, soon became one of the best-known Allied air units. It scored its first victory on 2 April 1916 and claimed its first Fokker on the twenty-fifth of that month, and from then on its tally rose steadily; in June 1916 its pilots destroyed 17 enemy aircraft, followed by 23 in July, 15 in August, 15 in September and 10 in November. On 23 November, however, Hawker was shot down by an up-and-coming German pilot named Manfred von Richthofen after a bitter, thirty-five-minute duel over Bapaume. A lucky shot creased Hawker's head, knocking him unconscious, and he crashed out of control. Richthofen later admitted that Hawker gave him the hardest fight of his career; had it not been for that single bullet, the Englishman might have gained the upper hand and the legend of the 'Red Baron' might never have been born.

New types of combat aircraft continued to appear in the air units of both sides during the spring and summer of 1916. From the spring of that year the task of overcoming the Fokker menace was shared, alongside the F.E.2b and D.H.2, by the Nieuport 11 single-seat fighter biplane, a type on which several British and French aces were to cut their teeth. The first Nieuport Scouts were received by Nos. 1 and 11 Squadrons early in March 1916. Armed with a single Lewis gun mounted on the top wing and firing over the propeller arc, the machines were found to have an excellent rate of climb,

BELOW The F.E.2, the first British fighter to challenge the Fokker E.III on the Western Front.

OPPOSITE TOP The highly successful D.H.2, seen here without its Lewis gun.

OPPOSITE BOTTOM A D.H.2 cockpit with Lewis gun mounted on the port side.

ABOVE The Nieuport 11 single-seat fighter biplane introduced on the Western Front in March 1916.

RIGHT A Nieuport 11 armed with two instead of the standard single Lewis gun.

LEFT Two French aces whose names became household words, Georges Guynemer with his Spad (*top*), and René Fonck, the top-scoring Allied pilot with seventy-five victories (*bottom*).

BELOW Albert Ball, a nineteen-year-old second lieutenant who scored forty-three victories before his death in 1917.

although their maximum speed of 96 mph left something to be desired and they had an unpleasant tendency to suffer structural damage during violent manœuvres. It took a very sure touch to get the best out of the Nieuport; one pilot who had it was a nineteen-year-old second lieutenant, formerly of the Sherwood Foresters, named Albert Ball. Ball's first posting in France was to No. 13 Squadron, flying B.E.2cs, but at every opportunity he used to visit No. 11 Squadron – which shared the same airfield – and borrow one of their Nieuports. At this time – June 1916 – No. 11 was engaged in attacks on enemy kite balloons, and Ball destroyed one of these in July. It was the first of forty-three victories that were to be scored by the young officer before his death in action in 1917.

During this period of bitter fighting several French pilots rose to fame like meteors. Foremost among them was Georges Guynemer, a frail twenty-year-

OVERLEAF A panorama of the Western Front by W. G. Wyllie.

old who had never enjoyed good health, yet who possessed a deadly degree of skill and marksmanship in the air. He scored his first victories in the summer of 1915 and went on to destroy fifty-four enemy aircraft before his death in action in September 1917. No one knows how Guynemer died; he and his aircraft fell in no-man's-land in the middle of a furious artillery barrage, and his body was never found.

Second only to Guynemer in popular appeal was René Fonck, who would become the top-scoring French pilot with seventy-five enemy aircraft to his credit. Whereas Guynemer often fought recklessly, attacking vastly superior numbers of enemy machines, Fonck was calm and calculating; he brought his own brand of science to air fighting, and it helped him to survive the war. Other French pilots whose names became household words were Charles Nungesser, René Dorme, Jean Navarre and Jean Chaput – all of whom survived the desperate battles against the Fokkers during the summer of 1915 to join the ranks of France's top-scorers.

By the summer of 1916 the Allied fighter squadrons were beginning to hold their own against the Fokkers. In the middle of the year two new Fokker types, the D.I and D.IV, began to appear over the front; they were designed to replace the E.III, but in fact fell far short of expectations. The Fokker D.I was no match in either climb or manœuvrability for the Nieuport, and before the year was out most of those supplied to units on the Western Front had been transferred to the less dangerous skies of the Russian Front. Germany's real hopes for regaining air supremacy lay with the Albatros D.I, which – armed with twin 7.92-mm Spandau guns and powered by a 160-hp Mercedes – made its appearance over the front in September 1916. It was the first German fighter to carry a two-gun armament without suffering a loss of performance, and although it was less manœuvrable than the Fokker types, it had better speed, climb and fire-power. In October 1916 an improved version, the Albatros D.II, also entered service at the front, and by the end of the year over two hundred were in service.

Another German fighter type that entered service in the summer of 1916 was the Halberstadt D.II, mounting a single Spandau and powered by a 120-hp Mercedes. Although highly manœuvrable and capable of holding a long, sustained power-dive, the Halberstadt was not a favourite aircraft among German pilots, most of whom seemed incapable of getting the best out of it. The notable exception was Oswald Boelcke, who flew both the Halberstadt and the Albatros and scored several victories with the former type. About a hundred Halberstadt D.IIs were in service by the end of 1916, but in the early part of 1917 they began to give way to the later Albatros variants. In December 1916 most of the thirty-four German Jagdstaffeln (Fighter Squadrons) on the Western Front had a mixed complement of Albatros and Halberstadt aircraft.

In February 1916 the Germans launched a massive offensive against the French at Verdun, precipitating one of the most prolonged and costly battles in the history of warfare. By the middle of the year the French defender of Verdun – General Pétain – was putting pressure on Sir Douglas Haig to open an early British offensive on the Somme. The broad object was to launch a relentless and sustained attack on the enemy over as broad a front as possible, weakening the Germans to such an extent that they would be unable to withstand the weight of French offensives planned for early 1917. The British Fourth Army was to spearhead the assault, advancing on Bapaume and then swinging southwards towards Ginchy; this move, combined with a simul-

ABOVE Anthony Fokker with his unsuccessful Fokker D.I, introduced on the Western Front in the summer of 1916.

taneous French attack on Sailly and Rancourt, was calculated to breach the enemy front between the Somme and the Serre. The British and French armies would then join forces and thrust forwards to Cambrai and Douai.

The opening of the Battle of the Somme at dawn on 1 July 1916 caught the German Flying Corps at a clear disadvantage. Air supremacy once more rested with the Allies, and the German squadrons at the front – which could muster only 129 serviceable aircraft between them compared with the RFC's 420 – were only just beginning to receive a trickle of new machines. During the first few days of the British offensive, therefore, it was the squadrons of the RFC that dominated the sky over the battlefield.

Their crews had a grandstand view of one of the greatest tragedies in the annals of the British Army. It was soon apparent that the infantry assault was not going according to plan. Everywhere along the line the advance was becoming bogged down; enemy machine-guns wrought terrible slaughter among the infantry as they stumbled over the churned-up earth, weighed down by extra entrenching equipment and blinded by the early morning sun as they desperately sought the gaps that the artillery was supposed to have torn in the German barbed-wire entanglements. The planners of the Somme offensive had apparently forgotten about the sun; it shone directly into the eyes of the attackers, its glare made more intense by a thin layer of mist, concealing the German positions as effectively as a smoke-screen.

Throughout the day – and the days that followed – the front line was constantly patrolled by the Martinsyde Scouts of No. 27 Squadron, the Moranes of No. 60, the F.E.2bs of No. 22 and the D.H.2s of No. 24. There were some isolated skirmishes, but the German Flying Corps was not yet in a position to offer combat in strength. For the most part, British and French reconnaissance aircraft were able to rove over enemy territory almost unmolested during the first two weeks of July.

The Battle of the Somme earned the RFC yet another Victoria Cross. It was won on the opening day of the offensive when Major L. M. B. Rees – a pilot with the newly arrived No. 32 Squadron, equipped with D.H.2s – sighted what he took to be a formation of British bombers returning from a raid over Festubert and climbed up to escort them home. It was almost a fatal error; the formation was German, and a few minutes earlier it had shot down another 32 Squadron pilot, 2nd Lieutenant C. J. Simpson. Rees soon found himself locked in a desperate fight with six enemy aircraft, one of which he shot down. Despite a wound in the thigh Rees continued to press home a series of determined attacks until the enemy formation suddenly broke off and flew back across the lines.

The German Flying Corps began to make its presence felt once more after 19 July, and two days later the D.H.2s of No. 24 Squadron had a stiff fight with a mixed formation of eleven Fokkers and L.F.Gs. The British pilots shot down four of the enemy aircraft for no loss to themselves. It was not until after the opening of the third phase of the Somme offensives on 15 September, however, that the Germans began to regain the initiative with the help of their newly formed Jagdstaffeln. Each Jagdstaffel was divided into two 'Schwärme' (Swarms) of six aircraft, which in turn were subdivided into 'Ketten' (Chains) of three machines each, corresponding roughly to the RFC's system of Flights and Sections. The first such unit was Jagdstaffel 2, commanded by Oswald Boelcke; Jagdstaffel 1 was never formed and existed only on paper. Boelcke assembled a band of promising young pilots – including Manfred von Richthofen, who had been flying two-seaters on the Russian Front – and subjected them to a period of intensive training. Those who already considered themselves competent pilots were in for a disagreeable surprise; in between learning to become proficient in handling the Jagdstaffel's new Halberstadts they were subjected to long sessions on the range with rifle and machine-gun, and Boelcke made them strip and reassemble their weapons until they could do it blindfolded. After every flight there were lessons on tactics and the strong and weak points of the Allied aircraft they were likely to meet in combat. Above all, Boelcke did his utmost to dispel the hatred for the British and French that wartime propaganda had nurtured in these young pilots, stressing continually that the Allied aircrews were skilled and courageous and that many were better pilots than himself.

The rigorous, incessant training went on for three weeks, during which time Boelcke flatly refused to send his pilots into combat. Boelcke himself flew intensively, adding to his score almost daily, and after every successful mission he would give his eager pilots a lesson in the tactics he had employed.

On 16 September Jagdstaffel 2 received the first dozen examples of the new Albatros D.I., and the following day Boelcke led his pilots into action for the first time. Not long after take-off the Germans sighted a formation of British two-seaters, with a fighter escort; they were eight B.E.2cs of No. 12 Squadron and six F.E.2bs of No. 11, on their way to attack a railway station at Marcoing, well behind the German lines. Boelcke manœuvred his formation until it was between the British machines and the lines, then closed in for the kill just as the B.E.s were attacking their objective. During the hectic air battle that followed Jagdstaffel 2 destroyed four F.E.s and two B.E.s. One of the former was claimed by von Richthofen. It crash-landed in a field behind the German lines. Von Richthofen landed alongside and helped German soldiers to pull the crew, 2nd Lieutenant L. B. F. Morris and Lieutenant T. Rees, from the shattered cockpit. Rees died almost immediately, Morris while on his way to a dressing-station. That night Richthofen wrote to a jeweller in Berlin, asking him to supply a small silver cup engraved with details of his victory. It was the first of eighty similar trophies.

During the days that followed, Jagdstaffel 2 went from strength to strength. It sustained the renewed German air offensive virtually single-handed until

ABOVE LEFT Manfred von Richthofen, the legendary 'Red Baron'.

ABOVE RIGHT Oswald Boelcke, commander of Jagdstaffel 2.

ABOVE A crashed B.E.2c.

more Jagdstaffeln reached the front during the first week of October, and accounted for a large proportion of the 123 Allied aircraft, most of them British, destroyed over the Somme during September. The Germans lost only 27 of their own aircraft during this period, and in October they destroyed a further 88 machines for the loss of 12 of their own. Boelcke himself destroyed 20 Allied machines during those two months, before his death late in October.

3 1917: The Killing Ground

During the winter of 1916/17 the problem of making good the severe losses suffered by the RFC during the previous four months seemed almost insurmountable. In an effort to fill the gap, the War Office ordered regimental commanders to appeal for volunteers for transfer to the RFC. Hundreds came forward, and at the same time the first Commonwealth volunteers also began to arrive. They were led by the Canadians, who, by special arrangement with the United States, had done most of their flying training in Texas and already possessed a high degree of skill.

The steady influx of these new personnel during the first weeks of 1917 did much to raise the morale of the RFC as it strove to gather its forces to meet the demands that would be imposed upon it by the coming spring offensives. The first of these involved a major French attack on the Aisne while the British pinned down a large part of the enemy forces in the north, the main objective in their sector being the capture of Vimy Ridge. The offensive began on 17 March 1917 and ended on 4 April. The First and Third British Armies were supported by twenty-five RFC squadrons, about half of them single-seat fighters. During the battle a new British combat aircraft, the Bristol Fighter, made its operational debut. A two-seater, it was equipped with a centrally mounted Vickers gun using the newly developed Constantinesco synchronization gear and a single Lewis gun on a Scarff ring in the rear cockpit.

The first squadron to equip with the type, No. 48, arrived in France towards the end of March 1917; it had only six Bristols on strength at the time of its arrival, and these were rushed into action before their pilots had got used to them. During their first patrol, on 5 April, six Bristols led by Captain Leefe Robinson, VC, encountered five Albatros D.IIs led by Manfred von Richthofen. The British pilots adopted the standard two-seater tactic of turning their backs on the enemy to allow their observers to bring their guns to bear. It was a fatal manœuvre and four of the six – including Leefe Robinson, who spent the rest of the war in a prison camp – were shot down.

Later, in an interview with a Berlin newspaper, Richthofen was openly contemptuous of the British machine, with the result that many German pilots came to regard the Bristol Fighter as easy meat – with fatal consequences to themselves. When flown offensively, in the same way as a single-seat fighter, it proved a superlative weapon and went on to log a formidable record of success in action. The man who perhaps did more than any other to vindicate the Bristol Fighter was a Canadian, Lieutenant Andrew McKeever, who joined No. 11 Squadron in May 1916. McKeever, who survived the war only to be killed in a road accident in 1919, destroyed thirty enemy aircraft while flying Bristols, and his observers shot down eleven more.

Another new type that closely followed the Bristol Fighter into action in the spring of 1917 was the S.E.5 single-seat fighter, which was delivered to

ABOVE Bristol F.2b fighters.

No. 56 Squadron in March. Powered by a 150-hp Hispano-Suiza engine, the aircraft had a maximum speed of 120 mph. Armament was a synchronized Vickers gun firing through the propeller and a drum-fed Lewis mounted over the wing centre-section. Although less manœuvrable than either the French-built Nieuports or Spads, the S.E.5 was faster and had an excellent rate of climb, enabling it to hold its own in combat with the latest German fighter types. The S.E.5s of No. 56 Squadron flew their first operational patrol on 22 April 1917, and it was while flying this type that Captain Albert Ball scored his final victories. One of his last air fights, on 2 May 1917, is described in the following combat report:

S.E.5 A.4855 [leader] on patrol with S.E.5 A.4854, at 13,000 feet at about 7.30 pm sighted four red Albatros Scouts, between Douai and the lines going south. S.E.5 A.4855 dived on the nearest red scout, but had four or five scouts coming down on his tail, so S.E.5 A.4855 turned steeply and pulled down his Lewis gun. Nearest HA [Hun Aircraft] fired at and overshot A.4855, and A.4855 put a good burst of fifty Vickers gun into HA. A.4855 then fastened on to the tail of HA and followed it down to 2000 feet, riddling HA meanwhile. HA dived into the rough ground between Halte and Vitry.

S.E.5 A.4855 turned and climbed and joined the scrimmage which was now taking place between a number of double-seater HA and HA Scouts, and Sopwith Scouts, Bristol Fighters and F.E.s. A.4855, circling and manœuvring for position, got on the tail of a white HA Scout with a pointed nose, and put in a good burst of Vickers. HA dived steeply and cleared. The mêlée gradually made towards Douai, HA being outmanœuvred and yielding ground. A.4855 went south to Cambrai and over Sailley viewed a white two-seater Albatros. A.4855 dived down on HA and put in a good burst of Vickers and a drum of Lewis from 100 to 25 yards range. HA hurtled down, but owing to the dusk [the time now being 8.10 pm] his ultimate end could not be observed . . .

Five days later, on the afternoon of 7 May, eleven S.E.5s of No. 56 Squadron set out on patrol. Only five came back, and Albert Ball, VC, was not among them. His end remains something of a mystery to this day; the Germans accorded the honour of shooting him down to Manfred von Richthofen's younger brother, Lothar, but in fact the latter was in hospital recovering from wounds on the day of Ball's death. The generally accepted version is that Ball was shot down by a German machine-gunner in the steeple of Annoeullin church as he flew low past it. The Germans buried him with full military honours.

RFC losses continued to mount steadily during the spring of 1917. There were three main reasons for the growing casualty rate. First, the RFC was still critically short of adequate combat aircraft; second, the prevailing westerly wind – which tended to carry the mêlée of air combat deep into enemy territory – was in the Germans' favour; and third, the RFC insisted on maintaining an offensive policy throughout, no matter what the cost.

TOP Captain Albert Ball in an early S.E.5 with enclosed cockpit.

ABOVE The cockpit of an S.E.5.

Faced with superior enemy aircraft, it inevitably suffered an increase in losses as a result of this. By April 1917 new pilots were being sent to the front with as little as seventeen and a half hours' flying experience, which precipitated a vicious circle: the more inexperienced the British pilots, the higher the success rate of the German fighter squadrons. By the middle of 'Bloody April' 1917 the average life expectancy of an RFC pilot in France had dropped to two months.

During the first week of April 1917 the RFC lost seventy-five aircraft in action – victims of an emerging band of tough, resolute German air fighters nurtured in the traditions of Boelcke and Immelmann. At their head was Manfred von Richthofen, and other German pilots were potentially just as dangerous to the Allies: men like Bruno Loerzer, the leader of Jagdstaffel 26, who destroyed 10 British aircraft during the Battle of Arras and who was to end the war with 45 victories. Then there was Werner Voss, the 'Hussar of Krefeld', who scored 12 victories in March 1917 and whose score at the time of his death later that year stood at 48; Erich Lowenhardt, who had 40 victories in the spring of 1917 and who went on to score 16 more; Karl Allmenroeder and Karl Schaefer, with 30 victories each; Kurt Wolff, with 27 at the time of the Battle of Arras; Otto Bernert with 26; and a host of other pilots who were to be numbered among the German Flying Corps's fifty top-scorers before the end of the war.

In accordance with the German practice of concentrating their best pilots into single crack units, most of the above-named men served with von

Vaux Wood

Sailly Saillisel

Lesboeufs

le Transloy

Maurepas   Bouchavesne

                Rancourt

 Pierre Vaast

                                    Combles   Le Foret Wood
                                        Bouleaux Wood   Leuze Wood

 Maurepas   Guillemont

                                            Ginchy

                                    Delville Wood

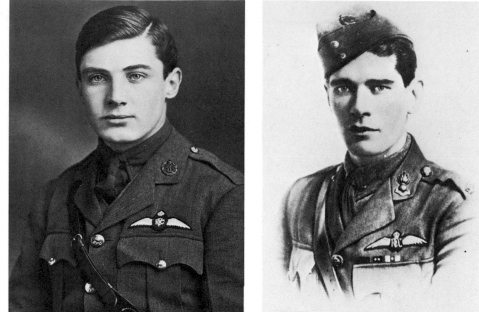

ABOVE Three leading British fighter aces, (*l to r*), James McCudden, Albert Rhys-Davids and Mick Mannock.

BELOW Roderick Dallas, a New Zealand ace.

OVERLEAF A view of the Western Front by W. G. Wyllie.

Richthofen's Jagdstaffel 11, which, in April 1917, was expanded into a Jagdgeschwader (Fighter Wing) consisting of three Staffeln (Squadrons). The Richthofen Jagdgeschwader – which soon became known, at least in the popular press, as 'Richthofen's Flying Circus' – was a highly mobile formation that could be shifted rapidly from one part of the front to another, wherever it was most needed. The RFC was forced to adopt a similar policy, concentrating its best fighter squadrons in opposition to von Richthofen wherever his squadrons appeared. These elite RFC units were the cradle of the leading British fighter aces. No. 56 Squadron, for example, in addition to Albert Ball, numbered among its ranks such famous fighter pilots as Captain James McCudden, who scored 58 victories before his death; Lieutenant Albert Rhys-Davids, who shot down Werner Voss; Captain Brunwin-Hales, with 27 'kills'; and Captain Henry Burden with 22. There was Captain W. A. Bishop of No. 60 Squadron, and later of No. 85, who survived the war as the second-ranking British fighter ace with 72 victories; he was narrowly beaten to top place by Major Mick Mannock, with a score of at least 74. Mannock flew with No. 40 Squadron, as did two other leading fighter aces: Captain G. E. H. McElroy, a Canadian with a score of 46, and Major Roderick Dallas, a New Zealander, with 39.

The number of British and Commonwealth pilots who scored 20 or more victories during the four years of conflict was fifty-three. Their combined score was 1,752 enemy aircraft destroyed – and, because of the rigid RFC system of confirming 'kills', the total may in fact have been much higher.

In June 1917 the British opened an offensive in Flanders, the main effort taking place in the Messines sector. The attack was supported by eighteen RFC squadrons with a total of 300 aircraft, about one-third of them single-seat fighters. On the first day of the offensive, 7 June, Captain W. A. Bishop of No. 60 Squadron was awarded the VC for destroying 4 out of 7 enemy aircraft in a daring single-handed attack on an airfield near Cambrai.

By the end of the month the RFC's reserves were sadly depleted, and the situation was further aggravated by the withdrawal on 21 June of two of its

LEFT Captain W. A. Bishop in a Nieuport Scout.

BELOW A Sopwith Camel, the first British aircraft fitted with twin Vickers guns. It first saw action in June 1917.

Sopwith Camel

best fighter squadrons, Nos. 56 and 66, for home defence. The latter consideration also helped to delay the re-quipment of RFC units in France with new aircraft – notably the Sopwith Camel, twenty-four of which were re-allocated to the air defence of Britain. The first examples did not reach France until July, when they were assigned to No. 70 Squadron.

For the RFC crews, stretched to their utmost during July, it was some consolation to know that von Richthofen was out of action for a time. On 6 July, forty fighters of the Richthofen Geschwader had attacked six F.E.2ds of No. 20 Squadron, escorted by four Sopwith Triplanes of No. 10 Squadron RNAS; two F.E.s were shot down, but an observer in another – 2nd Lieutenant A. E. Woodbridge – got in a good burst at Richthofen's red Albatros and sent it down to make a forced landing. Richthofen was wounded in the head.

The days before the Third Battle of Ypres, which opened on 31 July, were marked by intense air activity on both sides. At this time the combined strength of the RFC, RNAS, the French Aviation Militaire and the small Belgian Air Corps on the Western Front was 852 aircraft, 360 of which were fighters; the German strength was 600 machines, of which 200 were fighters. The air offensive began on 11 July, and on the first day fourteen German aircraft were destroyed for the loss of nine British. A few days later von Richthofen was back in action, his head still in bandages, and a series of massive dogfights took place between his Jagdgeschwader – consisting of Jagdstaffeln 4, 6, 10 and 11 – and Allied fighter formations. On the twenty-sixth, no fewer than ninety-four single-seat fighters fought one another at altitudes varying between 5000 and 7000 feet over Polygon Wood, and the following evening thirty Albatros and Halberstadt fighters attacked eight F.E.2ds over the same area. It was a trap; no sooner had the German fighters come down to intercept than they were savagely attacked by fifty-nine S.E.5s and Sopwith Triplanes. Nine enemy aircraft were destroyed for the loss of one S.E.5.

When the ground offensive began on the thirty-first much of the Allied effort was switched to attacks on enemy airfields and infantry columns with light bombs as well as machine-guns. During September the Allied fighter squadrons managed to maintain a substantial measure of air superiority. On the twenty-fifth, the RFC's fighter squadrons claimed nineteen victories for the loss of only one British aircraft. No. 56 Squadron, which had returned to France after only a brief stay in Britain, continued to be in the forefront of the

battle; by the end of September its score of enemy aircraft destroyed had risen to 200. This figure was matched, on 9 October, by No. 1 Squadron, now equipped with Sopwith Camels.

Then, just as the Allies were starting to gain the upper hand, there emerged a new and alarming development that was to have an enormous bearing on the conduct of the entire war. In November 1917 the revolutionary Bolshevik régime in Russia signed an armistice with the Germans. This meant that the hundreds of thousands of German troops, together with large numbers of guns and aircraft, which had been tied down in the war with Tsarist Russia could now be released for service on the Western Front. There was every possibility that the Germans would attempt a final massive offensive designed to smash the Allied armies once and for all in the early part of 1918, before American forces began to arrive on the Continent in large numbers.

As the year drew to its bloody close in the mud and carnage of Cambrai, Flesquieres and Bourlon Wood, it became increasingly clear that the real test would come in the spring of 1918 – and that air power would be the decisive factor.

4 1918: A Fall of Eagles

The expected German offensive on the Western Front was launched at 4.45 on 21 March 1918, with fifty-six divisions hurled against the fronts of the British Third and Fifth Armies. Despite all the preliminary warnings the attack, which was launched in thick mist, achieved total surprise, and by noon the German spearheads had smashed their way through the British defences.

As soon as the mist began to clear the RFC threw every available bomber and fighter into the assault against the densely packed enemy columns. Large-scale air battles flared up between the bomber escorts and German fighters, particularly on 23 March, when twenty-eight German aircraft were shot down for the loss of five British – although twenty-eight more British machines were lost in the course of the day through battle damage. The next day forty-two German machines were destroyed, and one Camel pilot of No. 43 Squadron, Captain J. L. Trollope, set up a record by shooting down six between dawn and dusk.

Although the low-level air attacks inflicted severe casualties on the advancing Germans the pace showed no sign of easing at the end of March. There was intense air fighting on 1 April; during the day seven aircraft failed to return from patrol and another from reconnaissance; two others were shot down while bombing Bapaume; twelve were damaged by anti-aircraft fire and crashed on landing; and twenty-four more were wrecked in other ways. The first of April 1918 followed the pattern of the endless days that had gone before it; aircraft going down in flames, faces missing from the mess-tents, exhausted crews, many of them unable to keep down any food except brandy and milk, snatching a few hours' nightmare-torn sleep before the dawn. To these men, hurling themselves into action day after day in support of the greatest fighting retreat in the history of the British Army, 1 April had no special significance other than that they had lived through it.

Fokker Dr.1

They were too busy fighting to realize fully that the Royal Flying Corps and the Royal Naval Air Service had fought their last battles. For on this first day of April 1918 the two arms were amalgamated and a new Service was born: the Royal Air Force.

There was to be no respite, no easy transition period for the new Service. The German offensive continued; by this time the fog had lifted and the new RAF was able to operate at maximum effort, with aircraft of every type ranging low over the front and attacking anything that moved with light bombs and machine-gun fire.

There was bitter fighting on 12 April, when the RAF flew more than 3200 hours on operations. Some crews were in action for five and a half hours between dawn and dusk. There were several big air fights, and Captain H. W. Woollett of No. 43 Squadron, flying a Camel, shot down six enemy aircraft before nightfall.

ABOVE A Fokker Dr.I triplane.

OVERLEAF 'Closing Up' by George Davis. Fokker Dr.I triplanes attacking a squadron of DH.4 bombers.

ABOVE No. 22 Squadron poses for
a photograph to mark the founding
of the RAF, 1 April 1918.

The British air activities contributed greatly to the overall defence, which
proved too strong for the Germans. Although they made several determined
efforts to extend their front during the week that followed, the British line
stood firm and the enemy offensive finally petered out.

There now followed a lull of four days in the fighting. During this period
the RAF kept up its attacks on the enemy rear areas and lines of communica-
tion, and reconnaissance aircraft kept the German positions under constant
surveillance.

On 21 April two R.E.8s of No. 3 (Australian) Squadron were photograph-
ing the lines west of Hamel when they were attacked by fifteen gaily coloured
Fokker Triplanes and Albatros D.IIIs. Their predicament was seen by
Captain A. R. Brown, leading eight Camels of No. 209 Squadron, who at
once went to their assistance. The Camel pilots were soon fighting for their
lives. One of them, 2nd Lieutenant W. R. May – a newcomer to the squadron,
carrying out his first operational patrol – exchanged fire with one enemy aircraft and then turned for home, as he had orders to avoid combat if possible.
Suddenly, machine-gun bullets crackled past his aircraft; looking round, he
saw an all-red Fokker Triplane hard on his tail. Roy Brown saw it too and
dived down to intervene. The three aircraft sped low over the front-line
trenches in line astern. Brown, two Australian machine-gunners of the 5th
Division and some Lewis gunners attached to a nearby Field Artillery battery
all fired at the red triplane simultaneously; it staggered, went down and
landed heavily on an even keel two miles inside the British lines. The pilot,

48

slumped in the cockpit, was dead; Manfred von Richthofen, after eighty victories in the air, had fought his last battle. Brown and the Australians each claimed the credit for shooting him down, sparking off a controversy which will probably never be satisfactorily resolved.

April 1918 was significant, too, for an entirely different reason. The month saw the operational debut of the first all-American combat unit on the Western Front: the First Pursuit Group, consisting initially of the 94th and 95th Squadrons. Most of the Group's personnel had served for some time with the Lafayette Escadrille and other French units, and some names were fast becoming legendary.

One of the most celebrated American pilots in France at this time was Major Raoul Lufbery, who trained the 94th Squadron to operational efficiency. It was not an easy task, for the aircraft used by the American Air Service in France were mostly second-rate French types – the French retaining the best machines for their own units – and serviceability was low. For this reason many American pilots preferred to stay with the French escadrilles rather than transfer.

Nevertheless, by the middle of April Lufbery judged that his pilots were ready to go into action, and on the eighteenth three Nieuport Scouts of the 94th Squadron were detailed to carry out the Group's first combat patrol. It was led by Captain David Peterson, with Lieutenants Reed Chambers and Edward Rickenbacker as his wingmen. The patrol was uneventful and the three pilots returned to their airfield. They had only just landed, however,

49

ABOVE Albatros fighters and
Martinsyde scouts over the Somme
in 1918.

when two German aircraft were reported in the vicinity. Two more American pilots, Lieutenants Alan Winslow and Douglas Campbell, immediately took off and each shot down an enemy machine – the first air victories credited to an American squadron.

The Americans learned fast during the weeks that followed, and victories began to mount. Tragically, Raoul Lufbery never lived to see his men reach their pinnacle of success: on 19 May, during a fight with an Albatros right over the 94th Squadron's airfield at Toul, his Nieuport was set on fire and spun earthwards, enveloped in flames. The American jumped clear and his body was found later in a garden on the outskirts of Nancy.

Two members of the First Pursuit Group went on to win America's highest award for gallantry – the Congressional Medal of Honor. The first was Lieutenant Frank Luke, who joined the Group's third squadron – the 27th – in August 1918. Luke quickly made a name for himself by shooting down enemy observation balloons, very dangerous targets which were usually defended by a ring of anti-aircraft guns. Luke seemed to bear a charmed life, and by 17 September 1918 his score stood at fifteen balloons and three enemy aircraft destroyed. A few days later, however, his luck ran out: he had just destroyed three more balloons in rapid succession when he was attacked by enemy aircraft. He shot down two of these and was racing for home when he was wounded by ground fire. He made a forced landing in enemy territory and fought off a squad of German soldiers for several minutes with his revolver before he was finally killed.

The second Medal of Honor winner was Major Edward Rickenbacker of the 94th Squadron, who before the end of the war was to shoot down at least twenty-six enemy aircraft – more than any other American pilot in the Great War. Rickenbacker achieved many of his notable victories at a time when the First Pursuit Group was battling against great odds and suffering heavy losses; in the summer of 1918, while still flying their elderly Nieuports, the American pilots now had to contend with the excellent new Fokker D.VII fighter, which had replaced the Fokker Triplane in service with the leading German air squadrons. In August 1918 alone, the German D.VII pilots destroyed no fewer than 565 Allied aircraft.

In the space of just a few weeks the First Pursuit Group lost almost all its best pilots – some of them killed when their overworked Nieuports broke up in the middle of a dogfight. Then, at last, the Group was re-equipped with more modern Spad fighters, enabling the Americans to meet the Fokkers on equal terms. Successes began to mount again, and in September 1918 there was keen rivalry between the 27th and 94th Squadrons – the latter now commanded by Rickenbacker – as each strove to capture the lead in shot-down enemy aircraft. For a short time the 27th jumped ahead, but Rickenbacker celebrated his appointment as commanding officer of the 94th by shooting down two German aircraft on the morning of 15 September, and during the coming week his pilots captured the lead once more. By the middle of October Rickenbacker had proved that the Spad in the hands of a capable pilot was every bit a match for the Fokker D.VII by shooting down twelve of these redoubtable enemy machines.

Two celebrated American pilots, Raoul Lufbery (*above*) and Edward Rickenbacker (*below*).

During the last months of the war the First Pursuit Group was joined in action by other American air fighting units; in all they numbered 700 pilots, over 100 of whom had served with the Lafayette Escadrille. Between them these pilots accounted for over 900 enemy aircraft; eighty of them destroyed five or more. The pilots of the First Pursuit Group alone shot down 285 enemy machines. It was no mean achievement for a fighting service which had entered combat three full years after its Allied contemporaries – and it laid a fine tradition which America's airmen were to sustain in a later conflict.

In August 1918 the Allied squadrons in France fought some of the greatest air battles of the war in support of a new offensive on the Somme, launched at dawn on 8 August on a line running from Albert to Hangard. The RAF bore the brunt of this fighting, and in the first thirty-six hours of the battle British airmen dropped 1,563 bombs and fired 122,150 rounds of ammunition against enemy ground forces. The German Jagdgeschwader, with their deadly Fokker D.VIIs, appeared in strength to challenge the Allied squadrons, and on the first day the RAF lost forty-five aircraft in action and another fifty-

ABOVE The excellent Fokker D.VII introduced in 1918.

BELOW Hermann Göring, commander of von Richthofen's Geschwader.

two destroyed through other causes. German losses were also severe; for example the Richthofen Geschwader – now commanded by Hermann Göring – which started the battle with fifty serviceable aircraft, was reduced to eleven after only a few days' fighting.

There was to be no respite for the exhausted pilots of either side during the last few weeks of the war. With the Germans retreating everywhere, the Allies continued to press their advantage, and support operations taxed the squadrons to their limit. The German Flying Corps, too, threw all its resources into the battle, with the Allied day bombers as its main target, and there was some fierce air fighting in October. On the thirtieth, sixty-seven enemy fighters were destroyed for the loss of forty-one British aircraft; many of the latter were de Havilland DH 9s and 9As, which – engaged in medium-level bombing attacks at between 10,000 and 13,000 feet – suffered heavily at the hands of the Fokker D.VIIs.

On 27 October one of the most remarkable battles in the history of air warfare resulted in the award of the RAF's last Victoria Cross of the First World War. That morning Major W. G. Barker – a Canadian pilot with No. 201 Squadron, flying a new Sopwith Snipe fighter – had just shot down an enemy two-seater reconnaissance aircraft at 21,000 feet over the Forest of Mormal when he was attacked by a Fokker D.VII and wounded in the thigh. The Snipe went into a spin, and when Barker recovered he found himself in the middle of a formation of fifteen Fokkers. He immediately attacked them, damaging two and shooting down a third before he was wounded again in the other thigh. The Snipe entered a second spin and this time Barker blacked out for a few seconds, regaining consciousness to find himself surrounded by another fifteen Fokkers. He shot down one of them, then a bullet shattered his left elbow and he again lost consciousness. When

he recovered he was immediately attacked by fifteen more German fighters; by this time his aircraft was belching smoke, and – convinced that it was about to catch fire – Barker dived at the nearest Fokker with the intention of ramming it. At the last instant he changed his mind and opened fire; the German fighter went down in flames.

It was Barker's fifty-third and last victory. Breaking off the unequal combat, the Canadian managed to get away and eventually crash-landed in the Allied lines. He recovered from his wounds only to be killed in a flying accident in March 1930.

Two weeks after Barker's exploit, on 11 November 1918, the guns on the Western Front were finally silenced.

ABOVE LEFT A Sopwith Snipe.

ABOVE RIGHT Major W. G. Barker.

53

5 Blitzkrieg – The Air War over Europe, 1939 – 40

At 4.00 in the morning of 1 September 1939 a code-word flashed out over the military communications network of the Luftwaffe High Command in Berlin to a score of airfields in eastern Germany. The code-word – *Ostmarkflug* – was the signal for the massive air-strike that was to precede Hitler's invasion of Poland.

At 4.45, fifteen minutes before the German armies rolled across the frontier, three Junkers 87 Stuka dive-bombers swept over the Vistula and bombed the railway line near the bridge at Dirschau, paving the way for the capture of this vital river crossing by an army task-force. The Stukas' bombs sparked off a holocaust that would only end six bitter years later, with half the world in ruins and over fifty million of its people dead.

The tactics used in the German assault on Poland involved, first of all, large-scale air attacks on Polish airfields and strategic positions, followed by armoured thrusts deep into enemy territory. Ahead of these armoured spearheads would go the dive-bombers, systematically clearing the way for the tanks and attacking communications, while overhead the Luftwaffe's fighters would deal with what was left of the Polish Air Force.

Such was Germany's concept of modern warfare. It was a concept that had a name: 'Blitzkrieg', or 'Lightning War'. It was a concept, moreover, that had already been tested and proved under operational conditions, on the bloody battlefields of the Spanish Civil War. When that conflict began in July 1936, both Germany and Italy lent their support to the Nationalist cause under General Franco, while the Soviet Government intervened on the side of the Republicans, and although the initial commitment was relatively small all three powers were to send men and material to Spain on a large scale over the three years that followed.

For Hitler's embryo Luftwaffe, born in defiance of the 1918 Treaty of Versailles – which forbade defeated Germany to have an air force – the war in Spain presented a golden opportunity to test the new combat aircraft and weapons secretly developed by the German industry since 1933. By the middle of 1937 the German commitment in Spain had grown to what amounted to a tactical air force, known as the Condor Legion and commanded by General Hugo Sperrle. His chief of staff was General Wolfram von Richthofen, cousin of the First World War ace.

It was in the Civil War that many of the Luftwaffe officers who were to rise to high command during the Second World War were blooded in combat: men like Werner Mölders and Adolf Galland, both of whom were later to command the German fighter arm. In Spain they led *Schlachtflieger* (ground attack) units, equipped initially with Heinkel He.51 biplanes. As the war progressed the Condor Legion received new combat types for operational trials in Spain; these included the Messerschmitt 109, which was to remain the backbone of the Luftwaffe's fighter force until 1945, the Heinkel 111 bomber, and the Junkers 87 Stuka dive-bomber. These machines enabled the

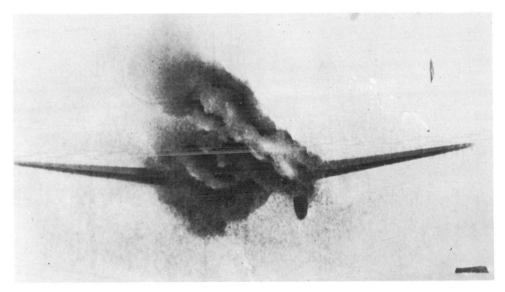

ABOVE LEFT The Junkers Ju 87B
Stuka dive-bomber.

ABOVE Adolf Galland, commander
of JG 26.

LEFT A Heinkel 111 bomber
catching fire in mid air.

BOTTOM LEFT The Junkers Ju 88A
medium bomber, one of the most
versatile aircraft of the Second
World War. It was used with
outstanding success as a dive-
bomber, ground-attack aircraft,
torpedo bomber, reconnaissance
aircraft, long-range fighter and
night-fighter.

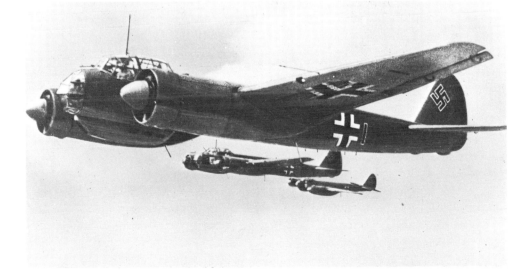

Nationalists to establish air superiority over the Russian types supplied to the Republicans, notably the I-16 Rata and I-15 Chaika, and the combat experience gained by the Luftwaffe pilots led to the complete revision of their air-fighting tactics.

At this time the world's air forces generally employed close wingtip-to-wingtip battle formations, and the Luftwaffe fighter pilots soon found that these were totally unsuited to combat because they hampered free manœuvring. They therefore evolved a new combat formation based on a pair of fighters, separated by about 200 yards, with the number two aircraft covering the leader's tail. Two pairs made up a *Schwarm* – later to be known as a 'finger four' by the Allies because the four aircraft formed a similar pattern to the spread-out fingertips of the right hand, palm downwards, and a squadron formation was made up of these sections of four, deployed down-sun at staggered altitudes so that all quarters of the sky were covered. These tactics proved greatly effective in Spain, especially when the Condor Legion's Messerschmitts were fitted with radio-telephony, enabling formation leaders to exercise full control.

By the time the Spanish Civil War ended in 1939 the Luftwaffe had developed its new tactics to a fine art; while its fighters swept the sky, its dive-bombers would blast a way ahead for the armoured divisions. Blitzkrieg had been born, and now, on this first day of September, Poland was to experience its full fury.

The first few hours of the German air offensive were marked by bad weather, which curtailed operations, but this cleared at noon and the Luftwaffe directed its main attacks against Polish troop concentrations. It was in the late afternoon that the onslaught began in earnest, with all twenty bomber groups of Luftflotte (Air Fleet) 1 carrying out heavy attacks on airfields, ammunition dumps, railway and factory installations and the Baltic ports. The Polish Air Force could do little to oppose the Luftwaffe's might; on the outbreak of hostilities it possessed about 450 aircraft of all types, including 140 fighters, and these were mostly obsolete PZL P.11s, which were completely outclassed by the Messerschmitts.

At 5 pm on 1 September three groups of Heinkel 111 bombers escorted by twin-engined Messerschmitt 110 fighters headed for the Polish capital, Warsaw. They were intercepted by two squadrons of PZLs; twenty-two aircraft in all against more than a hundred. The Polish fighters shot down two Heinkels and a 110, but five of their own number were also destroyed. Ninety minutes later the Luftwaffe attacked Warsaw once again; two more Heinkels were destroyed, but four PZLs were shot to pieces by the Messerschmitts. In less than two hours the two Polish squadrons had lost nearly half their aircraft. It was the same story with the Polish bomber squadrons; several of these carried out determined attacks on the enemy columns, but without fighter cover they were pounced on by the prowling Messerschmitts and massacred.

The Poles fought on. In the first six days of the battle the four PZL squadrons of the Pursuit Brigade, which was responsible for the defence of Warsaw, shot down forty-two enemy aircraft for the loss of thirty-seven of its own machines. The Poles' position, however, was desperate; apart from combat losses, more and more aircraft were being put out of action by the lack of spare parts and shortage of fuel. By 17 September, although its fighters claimed the destruction of 126 enemy aircraft, the Polish Air Force had lost 83 per cent of its machines and had practically ceased to exist as an effective force.

The Luftwaffe was now able to roam unopposed across the sky, and on 25 September wave after wave of German bombers systematically pounded Warsaw into rubble. Two days later, with no hope left, Poland capitulated. Yet the Polish contribution to the fight against Nazi Germany was only just beginning, for thousands of Polish soldiers and airmen who escaped before the final collapse were to fight on valiantly in the Allied cause until the end of the war.

When Britain and France declared war on Germany on 3 September 1939 both countries anticipated massive air attacks from the start of hostilities, but the waves of German bombers never came. It was RAF Bomber

ABOVE Bristol Blenheim bombers take off on a mission.

Command that struck the first blow, when ten Bristol Blenheim bombers carried out a daylight raid on the units of the German fleet in the Elbe estuary on 4 September. No significant damage was caused, and five Blenheims were shot down. Then, on 16 October, it was the Luftwaffe's turn: a formation of Junkers 88 dive-bombers of Kampfgeschwader (Bomber Wing) 30 attacked ships of the British Home Fleet in the Firth of Forth. The bombers were intercepted by the Spitfires of No. 605 Squadron and two of the Junkers 88s were shot down. On 18 December a further raid by the RAF on the German Navy at Wilhelmshaven – this time by Vickers Wellington bombers – ended in disaster; they were caught by two German fighter squadrons and half the attacking force of twenty-four Wellingtons failed to return.

Meanwhile, on the Western Front, the initial alarms that had followed the outbreak of hostilities had given way to the unreal period known as the 'Phoney War'. The British and French armies on the one hand, and the Germans on the other, settled in behind their defences to wait out the long winter months. Only in the air was there any real activity, as British, French and German fighters met in frequent skirmishes over the threatened borders. During these battles the Messerschmitt 109's performance proved to be superior to that of the British Hawker Hurricane and the French Morane 406 and Curtiss Hawk fighters. Thanks to a special carburation system the 109 could dive very steeply and carry out inverted manœuvres without its engine cutting out, which was not the case with the Allied fighters, whose fuel flow system worked by gravity. The Messerschmitt's armament of two cannon and two machine-guns was also superior to that of the Allied fighters.

The air fightings over the Western Front intensified during March 1940, leading to speculation that a German offensive was imminent. When the Germans struck, however, it was not in France that the first blow fell, but in Norway.

On the morning of 9 April 1940, in the wake of heavy bombing attacks,

LEFT The navigator of an He 111 in the cockpit.

German airborne forces occupied the key Norwegian airfields of Oslo-Fornebu and Stavanger-Sola. The Norwegians fought back hard, but under relentless enemy pressure they were steadily forced to yield ground. In an effort to redress the situation the Allies landed an expeditionary force of British, French and Polish troops at Namsos and Aandalsnes between 14 and 19 April; air cover for them was to be provided by eighteen Gloster Gladiator biplane fighters of No. 263 Squadron, RAF, which flew to a frozen lake at Lesjaskog from the aircraft carrier HMS *Glorious* on the twenty-fourth.

Conditions at Lesjaskog were fearful; nevertheless the Gladiators carried out regular patrols during the next three days and destroyed five enemy bombers before all but four of the British fighters were destroyed by enemy air attacks. The four survivors were destroyed by No. 263's personnel, who sailed for home on the twenty-eighth.

The squadron, equipped with fresh Gladiators, was back in Norway on 22 May, this time based at Bardufoss. During the next two weeks the Gladiator pilots destroyed at least twenty-one enemy aircraft, but on 7 June the Norwegian campaign came to an end with the Germans everywhere victorious, and the remaining Gladiators, together with a few Hurricanes of No. 46 Squadron which had also taken part in the battle, set course for the carrier *Glorious*. All landed safely, but as the *Glorious* was heading for Scapa Flow in the Orkneys she was caught in the open sea by the German battle-cruisers *Scharnhorst* and *Gneisenau* and sent to the bottom. With her, to her grave went the Gladiator pilots who had fought so gallantly against overwhelming odds.

At dawn on 10 May 1940, while the battle for Norway still raged, the Germans launched their offensive on the Western Front. Between dawn and dusk on this fateful day German bombers attacked seventy-two Allied airfields in Holland, Belgium and France. The Luftwaffe's main effort was directed against Holland, where airborne forces had the task of capturing vital strategic points and holding them until the 9th Panzer Division broke

TOP The wreckage of an He III shot down over Belgium.

ABOVE A flight of Hawker Hurricanes takes off for a patrol over France.

through. The German bomber formations were bitterly opposed by the Fokker D.21 fighters of the tiny Netherlands Army Aviation, but by noon on 14 May it no longer possessed any airworthy machines. The same was true in Belgium, where the Luftwaffe carried out seventy-five attacks on airfields during the first day of the invasion and destroyed thirty aircraft on the ground. They included nine Hawker Hurricanes and fourteen Gloster Gladiators, which represented the Belgian Air Force's most modern fighter types. By noon on 14 May the entire Belgian fighter force consisted of six Italian-built Fiat CR.42s, and these were evacuated to an airfield in northern France.

During the first three days of the invasion the British and French air forces carried out a series of desperate attacks on the enemy armoured

columns advancing through the Ardennes and across the Meuse bridges at Maastricht and Tongeren. Allied losses were fearful; on the first day alone the squadrons of the RAF Advanced Air Striking Force in France – equipped with Fairey Battle light bombers – lost twenty-three aircraft out of the sixty-four sent into action, and by the end of the second day the AASF's two squadrons of Blenheim bombers had also been wiped out. On the twelfth five Battles of No. 12 Squadron RAF made a suicidal attack on the bridges at Maastricht; all were shot down by the flak or the Messerschmitts.

On 14 May the Germans forced a crossing of the Meuse near Sedan, and the commander of the reeling French Army Group One asked the RAF to mount an attack on the enemy bridgeheads using every available aircraft. Sixty-three Fairey Battles were thrown into the cauldron; thirty-five failed to

ABOVE Pilots of No. 1 Squadron RAF race to their Hawker Hurricanes at a fighter aerodrome in France.

return. The French day-bomber force, too, suffered heavy losses, and by the end of 14 May was in no position to carry out further attacks.

Air cover for the German bridgeheads in the Sedan area was provided by three Wings of Messerschmitt 109s and one of Messerschmitt 110s. In all the German fighters flew 814 sorties on 14 May and claimed the destruction of eighty-nine Allied aircraft. Some of the German pilots flew as many as seven sorties before nightfall.

After the breakthrough at Sedan the German panzer columns raced across Belgium and northern France with shattering speed, driving for the Channel coast, and by 23 May it was clear that the Allied armies in Flanders – the Belgian Army, the French First Army and the British Expeditionary Force – were hopelessly trapped, with the BEF beginning its retreat to Dunkirk. On this day the panzers reached the Channel coast at Gravelines and swung northwards; twenty-four hours later they halted – partly because they had accomplished the major part of their mission and badly needed a rest, and partly because Hermann Göring, the Luftwaffe C.-in-C., had indicated that his airmen alone were capable of eliminating Allied resistance in and around the main evacuation ports.

The Luftwaffe in fact was in no position to do anything of the kind. The Stukas of Fliegerkorps VIII – which had supported the German armour in its dash through Belgium and France – were already badly overworked, and a large part of the Luftwaffe's medium bomber and fighter force was still operating from bases inside Germany. Since Dunkirk and the other ports were within easy reach of fighter bases in southern England, the Stukas could expect strong opposition – and their own fighter escort would be operating at the limit of its range.

The Stukas had a foretaste of things to come on 25 May, when fifteen of them were attacked by Spitfires over Calais. Four Stukas were shot down. The day after that the Luftwaffe carried out its first major attacks on Dunkirk; constant patrols were maintained over the port by sixteen Spitfire and Hurricane squadrons of No. 11 Group, RAF Fighter Command, whose pilots claimed twenty victories in the course of the day. In the air battles that raged over and around the beaches during the nine days of the Dunkirk evacuation the RAF lost 177 aircraft, and the Luftwaffe suffered a comparable loss. Although these losses were roughly similar on paper, the inescapable fact remains that the Luftwaffe had, for the first time, lost the

ABOVE Messerschmitt Bf. 109s,
unrivalled fighters in Poland and
France.

air superiority it had enjoyed since its attack on Poland the year before, and at the hands of RAF Fighter Command had suffered a psychological wound which, before long, was to be made deeper and more damaging in the skies over southern England.

After Dunkirk the Luftwaffe was heavily engaged in support of the German offensive across the River Somme against the French armies in the south, which fought on for another three weeks before the final collapse. The biggest air battle of this phase was fought on 3 June, when three huge formations of German bombers with a strong fighter escort – some 500 aircraft in all – carried out 'Operation Paula', a heavy raid on targets in the Paris area. The French put up every available fighter, but their efforts lacked co-ordination; there was no early-warning system and no real fighter control, and the enemy bombers often arrived over the French airfields before the fighters could take off. During the battle the French shot down twenty-six enemy aircraft; seventeen French fighters were destroyed in air combat and a further sixteen on the ground.

The French fighters battled on gallantly to the last, their efforts crippled by shortages of fuel, ammunition and spares, and the continual need to withdraw before the Germans overran their airfields. For most of them the armistice of 22 June came as a cruel blow; many made their escape to North Africa, where they carried on the fight as part of the Free French Forces.

And from Great Britain, which now stood alone against the might of Germany and Italy – the latter having declared war on the Allies on 10 June – the voice of Winston Churchill resounded through the free world: 'The battle which General Weygand has called the Battle of France is over. I expect that the Battle of Britain is about to begin . . .'

For the first time in history the fate of a nation would soon be decided by young men locked in deadly combat high above the earth, whose sacrifice would be marked by twisting vapour trails etched on a summer sky.

6 The Battle of Britain

In June 1940, while the Battle of France still raged, the Luftwaffe began to turn its attention to targets in the United Kingdom itself. Beginning on 5 June, German bombers operating in small numbers from bases in the conquered Low Countries struck by day and night at a series of 'fringe' targets along the east and south-east coasts of Britain. The raids, which lasted for about eight weeks, caused little significant damage – but they provided the Kampfgeschwader with invaluable operational and navigational experience for the bigger air onslaught that was to come.

On 30 June, a week after the end of the Battle of France, Reichsmarschall Hermann Göring issued a general directive outlining the Luftwaffe's aims in the projected air offensive against Britain. According to the directive the main target of the Luftwaffe was to be the Royal Air Force, with particular reference to its fighter airfields and aircraft factories. The German Admiralty, however, declared that the Royal Navy was just as important a target; it was vital that its dockyards and operational harbours should be put out of action at the earliest possible opportunity. Göring rashly stated that the Luftwaffe was capable of carrying out both tasks at the same time, but the Luftwaffe General Staff strongly disagreed and they had the last word. As long as the RAF remained unbeaten, the Luftwaffe's first priority must be to attack it by day and night at every opportunity, both on the ground and in the air, until it was destroyed. Then, and only then, would there be time to deal with other targets.

Although lacking in finer points of detail, the Luftwaffe's principal aim was now clear, and as a preliminary step towards achieving it Göring authorized his bombers to begin attacks on British convoys in the Channel early in July. The object of this move was not only to inflict serious losses on British shipping, but also to lure the RAF's main fighter forces into action. The first such attack on a large scale took place on 10 July, when a large formation of enemy bombers and fighters assembled over their airfields in the Pas de Calais to attack a convoy off Dover. They were detected by radar stations on the south coast, and a plot of their movements rapidly built up on the operations tables of Fighter Command HQ at Stanmore, No. 11 Group at Uxbridge and the Group's various sector stations.

The reaction of Air Vice-Marshal Keith Park, the officer commanding No. 11 Group, was cautious. Two hundred Spitfires and Hurricanes – about one-third of Britain's first-line fighter force – were under his command in nineteen squadrons, six of Spitfires and thirteen of Hurricanes, and he had no intention of allowing any of them to fall into an enemy trap. Six Hurricanes of No. 32 Squadron were already on patrol in the vicinity of the convoy, and to support them Park ordered twenty more Hurricanes and Spitfires – drawn from Nos. 11, 56, 64 and 74 Squadrons – into the air. By the time the latter arrived over the convoy No. 32's six Hurricanes were already in action against some seventy German aircraft – Dorniers and Messerschmitts – and a furious

RIGHT Messerschmitt Bf. 109s and Spitfires engage in a dogfight.

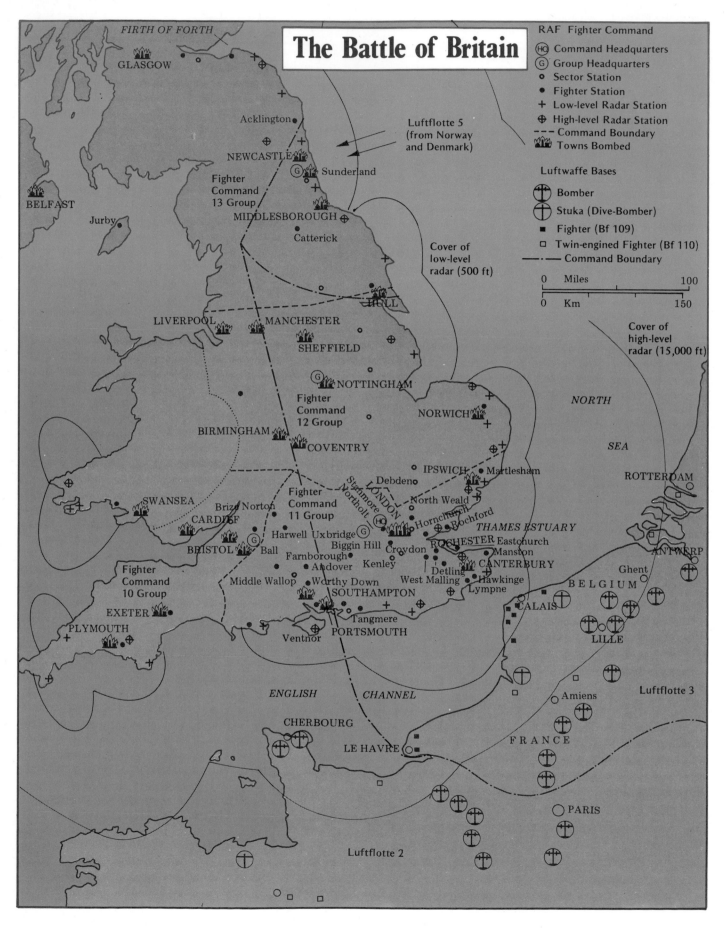

The Battle of Britain

RAF Fighter Command
- (HC) Command Headquarters
- (G) Group Headquarters
- ○ Sector Station
- ● Fighter Station
- + Low-level Radar Station
- ⊕ High-level Radar Station
- --- Command Boundary
- Towns Bombed

Luftwaffe Bases
- ⊕ Bomber
- ⊕ Stuka (Dive-Bomber)
- ■ Fighter (Bf 109)
- □ Twin-engined Fighter (Bf 110)
- —·— Command Boundary

Miles 0 ——— 100
Km 0 ——— 150

FIRTH OF FORTH

GLASGOW

Acklington

NEWCASTLE

Luftflotte 5 (from Norway and Denmark)

Sunderland

BELFAST

Jurby

Fighter Command 13 Group

MIDDLESBOROUGH

Catterick

Cover of low-level radar (500 ft)

LIVERPOOL   MANCHESTER

SHEFFIELD

HULL

Cover of high-level radar (15,000 ft)

NORTH

NOTTINGHAM

Fighter Command 12 Group

NORWICH

SEA

BIRMINGHAM

COVENTRY

Debden

IPSWICH   Martlesham

ROTTERDAM

SWANSEA

Brize Norton

Stanmore
Northolt

LONDON

North Weald

Hornchurch

Rochford

THAMES ESTUARY

ANTWERP

CARDIFF

Fighter Command 11 Group

Harwell Uxbridge

Biggin Hill

Croydon   ROCHESTER   Eastchurch

Ghent

BRISTOL   Ball

Farnborough

Andover

Kenley

Detling   Manston

CANTERBURY

BELGIUM

Fighter Command 10 Group

Middle Wallop   Worthy Down

West Malling   Hawkinge

LILLE

EXETER

SOUTHAMPTON

Tangmere

Lympne

CALAIS

PLYMOUTH

Ventnor   PORTSMOUTH

ENGLISH   CHANNEL

Amiens

Luftflotte 3

CHERBOURG

LE HAVRE

FRANCE

PARIS

Luftflotte 2

dogfight developed over the Channel. The Germans lost four aircraft, the RAF three, and one small coaster was sunk. The next day another convoy was attacked, this time by ten Junkers 87s of von Richthofen's Fliegerkorps VIII escorted by twenty Bf. 109s. They were intercepted by three Hurricanes of No. 501 Squadron and six Spitfires of No. 609 and in the ensuing dogfight the Germans shot down two Spitfires and a Hurricane for the loss of one Stuka. The convoy, however, escaped unharmed.

The convoy attacks continued during July and the first week of August. Although there were several major air battles during this phase, usually in the Dover area, the enemy formations were usually intercepted by only half a dozen British fighters, and were often able to carry out their attack and make for home before any fighters at all arrived on the scene. Despite the difficulties under which the RAF fighter pilots operated, however, they claimed the destruction of 186 enemy aircraft during this period for the loss of 46 Hurricanes and 32 Spitfires. Six Boulton-Paul Defiants of No. 141 Squadron were also destroyed in a single encounter with Messerschmitt 109s on 19 July, and after that the Defiant played no further part in the daylight phase of the battle. In four weeks of operations the Germans sent 40,000 tons of shipping to the bottom, and at the end of July the bombers inflicted a severe blow on the Royal Navy when they sank three destroyers off Dover and damaged a third in the space of forty-eight hours.

Hitler's hopes that Britain might be willing to talk peace, even at this late stage, were now dashed for good. It was clear that the struggle between Britain and Germany would be to the death – and by mid-July the Luftwaffe still had no firm operational plans for the great air offensive which, Göring believed, would be the instrument of a German victory. On 21 July the Reichsmarschall called the commanders of the Luftflotten (Air Fleets) together and ordered them to work out the details. Once again there were heated arguments among the General Staff. There was no doubt now that the destruction of the RAF was by far the most urgent task, but deciding exactly how best to achieve it as rapidly as possible was a different matter.

The plans had still not been finalized when, on 30 July, Hitler personally ordered Göring to put the Luftwaffe in a state of immediate readiness to carry out the attack. The primary aim, the Führer's directive read, was 'to destroy the flying units, ground organizations and supply installations of the RAF and the British air armaments industry'. The code-name for the air offensive was *Adler Angriff* – 'Eagle Attack'.

The organization which Fighter Command was now gearing up to meet the onslaught was very different from that with which the RAF had very nearly gone to war two years earlier, at the time of the Munich Crisis of 1938. Under the determined and energetic leadership of fifty-four-year-old Air Chief Marshal Sir Hugh Dowding, Fighter Command had become a tightly-knit defensive network where control and standardization were the keywords. There was no room for compromise in Dowding's character, and he was heartily disliked by more than one civil servant in the policy-making departments of the Air Ministry. Whatever Dowding wanted, he had to fight for all the way – and his stubbornness usually paid dividends. On one occasion, when he was fighting for the provision of bullet-proof windscreens for his Spitfires and Hurricanes, he destroyed his opposition with the simple observation that, 'If Chicago gangsters can ride behind bullet-proof glass I see no reason why my pilots should not do so too.' He got his windscreens.

Dowding's approach was essentially a scientific one; he believed that

ABOVE Air Vice-Marshal Keith Park, commander of No. 11 Group in the Battle of Britain.

ABOVE Air Chief Marshal Sir Hugh Dowding, head of RAF Fighter Command.

RIGHT The operations room at Fighter Command HQ in 1940.

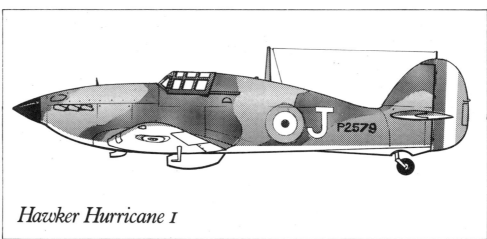

Hawker Hurricane 1

Britain's air defences should have the benefit of the latest technological developments. This was reflected in Fighter Command's operations rooms, linked with one another by an elaborate system of telephone and teleprinter lines to provide an integrated system of control. This enabled fighter aircraft to be passed rapidly from sector to sector and from Group to Group, wherever they were most needed.

Nowhere was modern technology more apparent in Britain's defences, however, than in the use of radar – or radio direction-finding, as it was then known. Developed by Robert Watson-Watt from earlier experiments in thunderstorm-detection by the use of radio waves, the use of radar as an integral part of the British air defence system was largely the fruit of Dowding's initiative; he had worked with Watson-Watt during the 1930s and had not been slow to recognize the potential of the new invention. The Germans had made several determined efforts to ferret out Britain's radar secrets before the war with the aid of special radio equipment installed in

ABOVE Supermarine Spitfires over the south of France from the film of *The Battle of Britain*.

commercial airliners and the airship *Graf Zeppelin*, but reconnaissance of this kind had come to a virtual standstill after the outbreak of war, and the erection of the radar chain along the south and south-east coasts of Britain had been allowed to continue unmolested.

Nevertheless, the destruction of the radar stations was recognized as a vital preliminary to the main air offensive against England. Planning for the offensive was completed by 2 August 1940; Luftflotten 2 and 3 were to attack simultaneously, their main task being to bring the British fighters to combat, to destroy the airfields and the radar 'eyes' on the coast, and to disrupt the RAF's ground organization in southern England. On the second day the attacks would be extended to airfields around London, and would continue at maximum effort throughout the third day. The Luftwaffe High Command hoped in this way to weaken the RAF by a few decisive blows, so establishing the air superiority necessary for any further operations.

To carry out this task the Luftwaffe had three Luftflotten. Luftflotte 2,

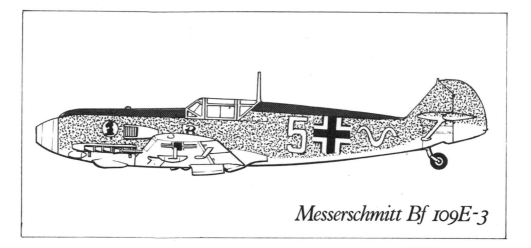

Messerschmitt Bf 109E-3

under Kesselring, was based in Holland, Belgium and north-east France; Luftflotte 3, under Sperrle, in north and north-west France; and Luftflotte 5, under Stumpff, in Norway and Denmark. Together their resources amounted to some 3500 aircraft, of which 2250 – 1000 medium bombers, 1000 fighters and 250 dive-bombers – were serviceable. To counter this force, Air Chief Marshal Dowding had 704 serviceable fighters, including 620 Spitfires and Hurricanes.

Everything was fixed except the date. To carry out its allotted tasks the Luftwaffe needed at least three days of continuous good weather. A fine spell was expected to continue during the first week of August, but the Luftflotten were unable to take advantage of it as they needed another week to make final preparations for the great onslaught. At last the Geschwader were ready and *Adlertag* – 'Eagle Day' – was fixed for 10 August, but then the weather took a sudden turn for the worse and it had to be postponed. On 11 August the weather-forecast for the new few days looked more promising; the final decision was made and *Adlertag* was scheduled for 13 August. H-hour was to be 7.30.

On the morning of 12 August, twenty-four hours before the main offensive was due to begin, twenty-one Messerschmitt 109s and 110s took off from Calais-Marck airfield and set course out over the Channel. They belonged to Special Group 210; the only unit of its kind in the Luftwaffe, its aircraft had all been fitted with racks enabling them to carry 500- and 1000-lb bombs. The previous day the Group had tried out the idea operationally for the first time when twenty-four Messerschmitts dive-bombed a convoy south-east of Harwich, setting two large transports on fire. The German aircraft had been intercepted by the Spitfires of No. 74 Squadron, but all had returned to base.

On this morning of 12 August Special Group 210's targets were the British radar stations at Dover, Pevensey and Rye. At 11.00 the Bf. 110s of the Group's No. 1 Flight dropped eight 1000-pounders on the Pevensey station, while the masts at Rye and Dover were attacked by Nos. 2 and 3 Flights. Although the bombs caused some damage, however, all three masts were operational again within three hours. It was a different story at Ventnor on the Isle of Wight, where the radar station was attacked thirty minutes later by fifteen Junkers 88s of Kampfgeschwader 51 and 54. Their bombing was extremely accurate and the station was damaged beyond repair. To cover up the dangerous gap created by the loss of the Ventnor station, the British

ABOVE Spitfires dive to attack German raiders during filming of *The Battle of Britain.*

transmitted a false signal on the wrecked station's frequency; the German listening-posts on the other side of the Channel consequently believed that Ventnor was still fully operational. In fact it was only after eleven days of non-stop work that another station was brought into action on the Isle of Wight.

While these attacks were in progress a force of Dornier 17s of KG 2 raided the airfield at Lympne with showers of 100-lb bombs, causing some damage to the tarmac, hangars and buildings. Attacks on British convoys in the Channel also continued; shortly after 12.00, twenty-two Junkers 87s of Lehrgeschwader 1 dive-bombed a convoy in the Thames Estuary north of Margate, scoring hits on two tramp steamers.

Then, at 13.30, it was once again the turn of Special Group 210. Twenty Messerschmitts swept over the airfield at Manston and dropped their bombs just as a flight of Spitfires of No. 65 Squadron was preparing to take off. The Spitfires got airborne amid the exploding bombs and climbed for altitude, but the Messerschmitts had gone – all except two, shot down by the airfield's anti-aircraft defences. Manston itself was temporarily put out of action. Later that afternoon the German bombers struck at Hawkinge and again at Lympne; both airfields were heavily damaged, and all through the night ground personnel worked like slaves to repair the cratered runways.

By nightfall on 12 August Luftflotten 2 and 3 had sent three hundred bombers – barely one-third of their total strength – against British targets.

The Luftwaffe had lost thirty-six aircraft, the RAF twenty-two; and the main offensive had yet to develop.

At 7.30 the next morning the Luftflotten stood ready to launch the onslaught, but at the last minute H-hour was postponed because of bad weather. The Dornier 17s of KG 2, however, failed to receive the signal in time; they took off in fog and rain and set course over the Channel without fighter escort. The fifty-five Dorniers were tracked by radar and Air Vice-Marshal Keith Park, commanding No. 11 Group, immediately 'scrambled' two squadrons of Hurricanes and a squadron of Spitfires, dividing them between the damaged airfields at Hawkinge and Manston and a convoy in the Thames Estuary. He also ordered most of a squadron of Hurricanes to patrol between Arundel and Petworth, leaving behind one section to cover their home base of Tangmere, near Chichester. Lastly, a squadron of Hurricanes orbiting over Canterbury could be called upon to support any of the other units engaging the enemy. Further west the commanding officer of No. 10 Group, Air Vice-Marshal Sir Quintin Brand, scrambled a squadron of Hurricanes to patrol the Dorset coast. Another squadron and a half of Hurricanes were held on immediate readiness at Exeter.

Flying in tight formation, just under the cloud-base, the Dorniers droned over Eastchurch airfield and unloaded their bombs on the runways, hangars and parked aircraft. At that moment the raiders were attacked by the Spitfires of No. 74 Squadron from Hornchurch, led by Squadron Leader A. G. Malan. One of the bombers dived vertically into the ground; the remainder climbed hard towards the clouds to escape the harrowing fighters. The battle was then joined by the Hurricanes of No. 151 Squadron, under Squadron Leader E. M. Donaldson, followed a few minutes later by the Hurricanes of No. 111 led by Squadron Leader J. M. Thompson, and a fierce air battle developed over the Thames Estuary. By the time the bombers reached the sheltering cloud three more of their number had gone down in flames.

At 11.30 twenty-three Messerschmitt 110s of Zerstörer-Lehrgeschwader 1 took off from their airfield near Caen with orders to patrol the south coast of England near Portland. Although they were picked up by radar as they crossed the French coast near Cherbourg, and although their strength was correctly reported as 'twenty plus bandits', there was one thing the radar 'eye' could not tell: the type of aircraft. Since Dowding had given orders that his Spitfires and Hurricanes were to avoid combat with enemy fighters if possible, and concentrate on the bombers, the sector controllers of No. 11

OPPOSITE TOP A Hawker Hurricane.

OPPOSITE BOTTOM A Messerschmitt Bf. 109 attacks a Spitfire with lethal accuracy.

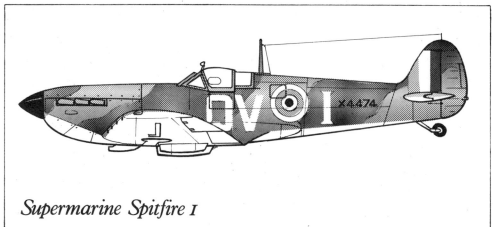

Supermarine Spitfire I

Group would probably not have scrambled any fighter squadrons had they known the identity of the enemy aircraft. In the event, three Hurricane and Spitfire squadrons took off from Tangmere, Warmwell and Exeter to intercept the enemy, and in doing so fell into the very trap Dowding had been trying to avoid. The Germans planned that when their bombers finally arrived they would catch the Spitfires and Hurricanes on the ground as they refuelled and rearmed.

The Hurricanes engaged the Bf. 110s over the coast and the German fighters immediately adopted a defensive circle. Three Hurricanes were forced to break off the action with battle damage, but five 110s went down into the sea, and several score were so badly damaged that they were out of action for a number of days. The action highlighted the heavy, twin-engined Bf. 110s inferiority in combat with lighter, more manœuvrable fighters, and to make matters worse Lehrgeschwader 1's mission had failed. The unit had drawn three British fighter squadrons on to itself so that the bombers could slip through according to plan – but the bombers did not come for another three hours, by which time the RAF fighter squadrons were ready for them once more.

At 15.00 fifty-two Junkers 87s of Stuka-Geschwader 77 under Major Graf Schönborn took off from their base at Flers to attack RAF airfields near Portland. They were escorted by the Messerschmitt 109s of Jagdgeschwader 27. However, southern England was hidden under a blanket of cloud, making a dive-bombing attack out of the question, and the Stukas circled over the coast in search of a target. Within minutes their fighter escort was being hotly engaged by a strong force of Hurricanes from Exeter and Middle Wallop, while fifteen Spitfires of No. 609 Squadron attacked the bombers. Five of the Stukas were quickly shot down; the remainder fled for home, still carrying their bombs.

The next wave of bombers, approaching the coast a few minutes later, ran into the hornets' nest stirred up by Stuka-Geschwader 77. They were the Junkers 88s of Lehrgeschwader 1, and they used the cloud cover to good advantage. One formation dropped their bombs on Southampton harbour, while six more Junkers 88s dived on the airfield at Middle Wallop, one of Fighter Command's vital sector stations. Their bombs caused only light damage, but severe damage was inflicted by another Ju. 88 formation at Andover, a few miles away.

Meanwhile, further east, over Kent, No. 11 Group was having a hard time of it. General Loerzer's Fliegerkorps II had sent in both its Stuka-Geschwader, as well as a third from Fliegerkorps VIII, preceded by the Bf. 109s of JG 26. The Messerschmitts were able to beat off a flight of Spitfires from Kenley, allowing the eighty-six Junkers 87s to proceed unmolested to their target, the airfield of Detling near Maidstone. Fifteen minutes later the airfield lay in ruins; the hangars were burning, the operations room was wrecked, the station commander was dead and twenty British aircraft were destroyed. It was a brilliant attack, and in terms of its execution was highly successful. But there were no RAF fighters at Detling; it was a Coastal Command station.

So 'Eagle Day' drew to a close. In spite of the bad weather and the abortive start to the assault, the Luftwaffe bombers had flown 485 sorties and the fighters' thousand combat reports at the end of the day claimed that nine enemy airfields had been attacked, 'five with such great success that they could now be regarded as unserviceable'. Field-Marshals Kesselring

ABOVE A Messerschmitt Bf. 110. These aircraft participated with little success in the Battle of Britain and over 200 were shot down. This photograph shows an early prototype.

and Sperrle were well satisfied with the day's work, although it had been paid for with the loss of thirty-four bombers and eleven fighters. It had, however, not been the decisive blow they had anticipated. On the other side of the Channel, too, 13 August had been hailed as a success by the RAF. It was true that three airfields had been badly damaged, but not one of them was a fighter base. The RAF's loss was thirteen aircraft and seven pilots.

The Luftwaffe's plans were also frustrated by bad weather on 14 August. The only major raid was carried out by sixteen Bf. 110s of Special Group 210, which attacked Manston, but apart from that the Luftwaffe sent over its bombers in small numbers to keep the British defences in a state of alert.

At 10.30 on 15 August patches of blue sky began to show through the grey overcast which had stretched from horizon to horizon since dawn, and by 11.00 the clouds had broken up completely. A few minutes later forty Stukas of Fliegerkorps II, escorted by a similar number of Bf. 109s, crossed the French coast near Cap Blanc Nez. Their targets were the airfields of Lympne and Hawkinge. As they turned over the British coast they were met by the Spitfires of Nos. 54 and 501 Squadrons, but these were held at bay by the 109s, and the Stukas caused severe damage at Lympne, putting the airfield out of action for two days. The damage was less severe at Hawkinge, where one hangar was hit and a barrack-block destroyed.

The scene of the battle now shifted further north, and it was the turn of General Stumpff's Luftflotte 5. It was the first time that Luftflotte 5 had been committed in a large-scale attack on England, and the German pilots faced their task with many misgivings. Range was the biggest problem. Both Kampfgeschwader – KG 26 and KG 30 – had to fly between 400 and 450 miles from their bases at Stavanger in Norway and Aalberg in Denmark before reaching their targets along the north-east coast between the Tyne and Humber estuaries. Altogether they had to cover a distance of some 1200 miles, carrying a 20 per cent reserve of fuel to allow for take-off and landing, navigational errors and loiter over the target. Also, the distance was too great for the bombers to be escorted by single-engined Bf. 109s. For this mission they used 110s – a far from ideal state of affairs, as had already been proved.

ABOVE A Spitfire viewed through a Heinkel 111 gun turret.

Stumpff's only hope of success was that the heavy fighting in the south might have prompted Dowding to move a large part of his fighter reserves from the north to reinforce the hard-pressed Nos. 10 and 11 Groups. But Dowding knew the importance of rotating his squadrons and resting his battle-weary pilots, and the RAF's order of battle was much the same as it had been on 13 August.

The radar stations on the east coast picked up the first wave of incoming bombers when it was still far out over the North Sea. It was 13.30, and this first wave consisted of sixty-three Heinkel 111s of KG 26, escorted by twenty-one Bf. 110s of ZG 76. The twelve Spitfires of No. 72 Squadron, led by Flight Lieutenant Ted Graham, were scrambled from Acklington to intercept and climbed hard over the Farne Islands. Thirty miles off the coast one of the pilots sighted the enemy armada and told Graham, asking whether the latter had seen the mass of aircraft spread out across the sky. 'Yes, I see them,' replied Graham. 'I was just wondering what to do!'

He did not hesitate for long. Bringing the squadron round in a wide turn, climbing all the time, he manœuvred into position for an attack out of the sun. His amazement at seeing so many bombers was understandable. For the past forty minutes the radar had been estimating the strength of the raid at 'thirty plus', flying on a southerly course. In fact the radar was not to blame in this case, because the first formation it had detected was not KG 26 at all, but consisted of twenty Heinkel 115 seaplanes which had been sent towards the Firth of Forth as a diversion. The targets assigned to KG 26

78

lay a considerable distance further south; they were the bomber airfields of Dishforth and Linton-on-Ouse, in Yorkshire. KG 26, however, had made a navigational error; the bombers and their escort had made landfall a hundred miles up the coast, and had turned into the path of the diversionary seaplanes.

No. 72's Spitfires, now joined by the Hurricanes of No. 79 Squadron, also from Acklington, sailed into the attack and the Messerschmitt 110s were soon fighting for their lives. The bombers continued southwards, searching for their targets; the first wave, harried by a flight of No. 79 Squadron Hurricanes, a flight of No. 605 Squadron Hurricanes which had come down from Drem, and the anti-aircraft guns along the Tyne, unloaded its bombs at random along the coast between Newcastle and Sunderland. The second wave, engaged by the Spitfires of No. 41 Squadron from Catterick and the Hurricanes of No. 607 Squadron from Usworth, dropped its load near Sunderland. KG 26's part in the raid had ended in failure; eight Heinkels and six Bf. 110s had been shot down.

Meanwhile, under cover of KG 26's movements the Junkers 88s of KG 30 were coming in towards Flamborough Head. While they were still a long way out to sea warning of their approach was received in the operations room of No. 12 Group at Watnall, and the raid strength was estimated at thirty plus. Air Vice-Marshall Trafford Leigh-Mallory, commanding No. 12 Group, ordered eighteen Spitfires and Hurricanes of Nos. 616 and 73 Squadrons up from Church Fenton to intercept the raiders. The Spitfires met the fifty Ju. 88s while they were still out to sea, and the Hurricanes at-

ABOVE Air Vice-Marshal Trafford Leigh-Mallory, commander of No. 12 Group.

tacked them as they crossed the coast. Nevertheless, the majority of the German formation reached their target – Driffield, an airfield in No. 4 (Bomber) Group – and destroyed four hangars as well as several Whitley bombers. Six of the Ju. 88s were shot down.

The rest had hardly droned away when, in the south, the battle flared up once more. At 15.00, the Dornier 17s of KG 3 took off from St Trond and Antwerp-Deurne, in Belgium. Over the coast they made rendezvous with their fighter escort: the Messerschmitt 109s of JGs 26, 51, 52 and 54. The German formation was detected by radar as it assembled over Belgium and northern France, and as it headed out over the Channel eleven RAF fighter squadrons – about 130 Spitfires and Hurricanes – were hurriedly scrambled. Such was the diversity of the incoming raid plots, however, that the fighters were shuttled backwards and forwards by the sector controllers with no real co-ordination. For example, the Hurricanes of No. 17 Squadron were patrolling the Thames Estuary when suddenly they received an urgent recall to their base at Martlesham Heath, north of Harwich. While still a long distance away the pilots could see tall columns of smoke rising from Martlesham, and when they arrived overhead they found that the airfield had been badly hit. Unnoticed and without any opposition whatsoever, Special Group 210's twenty-four bomb-carrying Messerschmitts had slipped in at low level, bombed, and vanished before anyone had a chance to fire a shot. It was thirty-six hours before the field could be made serviceable once more.

Meanwhile, the Dorniers of KG 3 had split into two waves, one heading for Eastchurch and the other for Rochester. At the latter field their bombs caused severe damage to the Short aircraft factory, setting back production of the Stirling four-engined bomber by several months.

So far, Kesselring's Luftflotte 2 had been attacking across the Straits of Dover. Now it was Sperrle's turn; 120 miles further to the south-west his units were already forming up over their airfields. At 16.45 the Junkers 88s of LG 1 took off from Orleans, followed fifteen minutes later by the Junkers 87s of StG 1 from Cherbourg. The bombers rendezvoused with the Bf. 109s of JG 26 and JG 53 and the Bf. 110s of ZG 2, and at 18.00 the whole armada of more than two hundred aircraft set course towards the British coast.

The Germans, however, had thrown away their tactical advantage; the time elapsing between their raids had enabled Air Vice-Marshals Park and Brand to take adequate counter-measures, and to meet the attackers they were able to put up an umbrella of fourteen fighter squadrons – a total of 170 aircraft. This was the biggest number of fighters that the British had so far committed to the battle at any one time. The Spitfires and Hurricanes met the bombers over the coast and concentrated on the Stukas, which were soon fighting desperately for survival. Under cover of the *mêlée* the Junkers 88s of LG 1 tried to slip through to their targets, but the Spitfires were soon upon them and one Junkers 88 after another went down in flames. Out of the fifteen aircraft of LG 1's No. 2 Squadron, only three managed to reach their target – the Fleet Air Arm base at Worthy Down, north-east of Southampton. The others – those that were left – jettisoned their bombs and fled for home. Even worse hit was the Geschwader's No. 4 Squadron, whose No. 2 Flight lost five aircraft out of seven.

LG 1's No. 1 Squadron was more fortunate. Its twelve Junkers 88s had been the first to cross the coast, and had managed to achieve an element of surprise. They dived on Middle Wallop, just a fraction too late to catch two fighter squadrons on the ground. The last Spitfires of No. 609 Squadron were just taking off when the bombs exploded among the hangars. It was the third raid on Middle Wallop in three days. During the attack the German pilots had the impression that they were bombing Andover; apparently they still did not know that Middle Wallop was a much more important sector station.

The thunder of engines died away and there was a brief lull in the fighting. The anti-aircraft gunners cleared away the piles of empty shell cases, sweating ground crews toiled to refuel and rearm the Spitfires and Hurricanes. The battle-weary pilots snatched a few minutes respite and wondered: what next?

They were not kept waiting for long. At 19.35 fifteen Bf. 110s and eight Bf. 109s of Special Group 210 set course over the Channel, escorted by the 109s of JG 52. Their target was Kenley, south of London, but they made a navigational error and bombed Croydon by mistake, destroying forty training aircraft. As they were carrying out their attack they were intercepted by the Hurricanes of Nos. 32 and 111 Squadrons and four Bf. 110s were quickly shot down. The remainder ran for the Channel, but over the coast they were attacked by the Spitfires of No. 66 Squadron and two more 110s went down. One Bf. 109 also failed to return from this mission, bringing Special Group 210's loss to seven aircraft.

As night fell on 15 August both sides retired to lick their wounds and assess

BELOW A Heinkel 111 makes for home with its starboard engine smoking.

their victories and losses. The Luftwaffe had flown 1,270 fighter and 520 bomber sorties during the day, and the Germans had lost 75 aircraft – mostly bombers and Bf. 110s. The RAF's loss was 34, although the Luftwaffe claimed that 111 RAF fighters had been shot down. Admittedly, the British loss only included those machines which were totally destroyed; a Spitfire or Hurricane which had to make a forced landing but stayed largely in one piece was classed as repairable even though it might be out of action for weeks. Yet the German pilot who shot it down and saw it crash-land would naturally claim it as a 'kill'. Furthermore, if a British fighter attacking a German bomber formation was seen to crash, in all probability at least half a dozen gunners would claim that they had shot it down. The Americans had the same problem in assessing their daylight bomber crews' claims, later in the war, over France and Germany.

During the bitter fighting of those August weeks RAF Fighter Command was losing more aircraft than could be replaced, although the aircraft industry had been working flat out for several months. On 11 May 1940 Winston Churchill – newly Prime Minister – had appointed Lord Beaverbrook to the post of Minister of Aircraft Production. The 'Beaver' stirred up a lot of dust in bureaucratic military circles; using the same methods by which he had built up his newspaper empire, he bludgeoned the aircraft industry into reaching a new level of production. By June 1940 production had reached between 440 and 490 aircraft a month, most of them fighters, and the flow hardly decreased even under the pressure of the German air attacks. In contrast, German figures for the production of, for example, the Messerschmitt 109 were poor. In June 1940 the factories turned out 164 Bf. 109s, in July 220, in August 173 and in September 218. This meant that during the months of crisis the Luftwaffe was not receiving half as many fighter aircraft as its opponent. The German fighter pilots were well aware of the situation and raised their voices in protest, but in vain. It was not until late 1942 – with the start of the heavy American daylight raids on German-occupied territory – that fighter production took a big leap upwards. By that time it was too late; the tide of the air war had already turned.

On 16 August the Luftwaffe returned to England in force and struck at Brize Norton, Manston, West Malling, Tangmere, Gosport, Lee-on-Solent, Farnborough and Harwell. Forty-six training aircraft were destroyed at Brize Norton, and the radar station at Ventnor on the Isle of Wight was bombed once more.

Shortly before noon Flight Lieutenant J. B. Nicolson of No. 249 Squadron was patrolling near Southampton when his Hurricane was attacked by a Messerschmitt 110. Cannon-shells wounded Nicolson in the leg and eye and set his aircraft on fire, yet he remained in the blazing cockpit and managed to shoot down his attacker before bailing out, severely burned. He was awarded the Victoria Cross, the only one to be won by a fighter pilot during the Second World War.

In the afternoon of 16 August the weather clamped down once more. Luftflotte 2 sent out a force of bombers to attack the fighter airfields of Debden, Duxford, North Weald and Hornchurch, but the raiders returned to base with their bombs still on board, unable to find their targets through a thick blanket of cloud. At the day's end the Luftwaffe had lost forty-five aircraft in combat against the RAF's twenty-two. The following day was remarkable only for its complete lack of action; both sides welcomed the respite, short-lived though it was.

OPPOSITE Messerschmitt Bf. 109s from *The Battle of Britain*. The 109s used in the film were ex-Spanish Hispano IIA-1109s with Rolls Royce Merlin engines.

On Sunday, 18 August, KG 76 launched a series of heavy attacks on the sector stations of Kenley and Biggin Hill. Kenley was severely hit, and its all-important operations room badly damaged. Shortly before 13.00 the Hurricanes of No. 615 Squadron took off from Hawkinge to intercept a force of incoming bombers. Instead, they encountered a superior number of Bf. 109s and took a severe mauling.

It was the Junkers 87s, however, which suffered most heavily on this Sunday afternoon. Four Stuka Gruppen from Fliegerkorps VIII attacked the airfields at Ford, Gosport and Thorney Island, together with the radar station at Poley on the south coast. With inadequate fighter escort, they ran into the Hurricanes of 43 and the Spitfires of 152 Squadrons, which literally shot them to pieces. When at last they droned away over the Channel, they left behind the blazing wrecks of thirty of their number. It was the last time that the Stuka appeared in British skies; the dive-bomber casualties accounted for nearly half the total Luftwaffe loss – seventy-one aircraft – on 18 August. The RAF lost twenty-seven fighters.

August 23 saw the radar station at Ventnor – shattered by Special Group 210 on the twelfth – back in operation again. The weather continued to improve steadily, and the Luftwaffe resumed its attacks on RAF ground installations. The next day North Weald was heavily bombed, and Hornchurch escaped with only a relatively light attack. The Luftwaffe stepped up its assault once more during the last week in August, striking again and again at the RAF airfields lying in a defensive semi-circle before London: Kenley, Redhill, Biggin Hill, West Malling, Detling and Gravesend to the south-east; Hornchurch, Rochford, Debden and North Weald to the north-east. On the thirtieth Biggin Hill was completely wrecked, with sixty-five personnel killed and wounded. The worst damage was done by only eight Dornier 17s of KG 76, attacking at low level.

Biggin Hill was hit yet again on the afternoon of 31 August, this time by the Dorniers of KG 2. A second force of Dorniers swept over Hornchurch and released their bombs right on top of No. 54 Squadron's Spitfires, which were taxying out for take-off. The last flight, led by Squadron Leader Al Deere, was blown apart by a stick of bombs just as it was getting airborne. The three Spitfires were completely wrecked, but miraculously the pilots escaped with only minor injuries. The Biggin Hill squadrons – Nos. 72 and 79 – were luckier; they were already airborne, and patrolling well to the south, when the bombers hit the airfield. Nevertheless, 31 August had been a tough day for Fighter Command; thirty-two Spitfires and Hurricanes had been destroyed, against thirty-nine enemy aircraft.

The position was beginning to look black for the RAF. By the first week of September the British losses were so high that there were not enough replacement pilots to fill the gaps. In the fourteen days between 24 August and 6 September the RAF lost 103 pilots killed and 128 badly wounded – almost a quarter of the total number of trained fighter pilots.

To make matters worse, the Germans were tightening up their fighter escort procedure. On 1 September, when KG 1 attacked the docks at Tilbury, its eighteen Heinkel 111s were escorted by three Jagdgeschwader – roughly four fighters to every bomber. All the German aircraft returned to base without loss, having been virtually unmolested by the RAF. It was the same on 2 September; for the first time since the battle began, a Messerschmitt 110 Geschwader – ZG 76 – was able to carry out an unopposed escort mission over southern England. The pilots, who were escorting KG 53 in a

raid on Eastchurch, reported that they had not seen a single RAF fighter in the air. The lack of opposition lent fresh courage to the Luftwaffe pilots; at least it looked as though the final collapse of Fighter Command was imminent.

ABOVE A Dornier Do 17 bomber, nicknamed the 'Flying Pencil' because of its long thin shape.

But unknown to the ordinary aircrews, decisions were already being made which, ultimately, would tip the scales in the RAF's favour. On 3 September Göring summoned Field-Marshals Sperrle and Kesselring to a meeting at the Hague. There he told them that Hitler was pressing him to switch the main attacks on to London itself, as a reprisal for RAF raids on Berlin. Following a brief – and erroneous – raid on London by KG 1 on the night of 24 August, RAF Bomber Command had struck at the German capital four times in the succeeding ten days. Damage had been negligible, but Hitler had vowed reprisals. Sperrle bitterly opposed any plan to switch the attacks away from the British airfields at this crucial stage of the battle. Kesselring, on the other hand, believed that the RAF was on the point of evacuating the hard-hit forward airfields and withdrawing to bases west of London, beyond the range of the escorting German fighters. In this case, Kesselring argued, the only sure way of destroying RAF Fighter Command was to overwhelm it in air combat. If the Luftwaffe mounted a large-scale assault on London, the RAF would be forced to throw its last fighter reserves into the defence of the capital. So Kesselring believed – and the force of his argument finally convinced Göring. The die was cast, and London's agony was about to begin.

On the night of 5 September seventy bombers unloaded sixty tons of bombs on the London docks. Two days later, from 15.00 in the afternoon of 7 September until dawn the following day, a mighty armada of 625 bombers, escorted by as many fighters, hit the docks in an almost non-stop assault. The whole of the docks area was one burning beacon, guiding the night bombers unerringly to their target. Yet when morning came it was 'business as usual' in the streets of the great city. Under a pall of smoke, London licked her

ABOVE The He III medium bomber – a Spanish Air Force version with Rolls Royce Merlin engines.

wounds, shook herself like an angry old dog and raised her head once more in defiance.

The real test, however, was still to come. On 15 September the Luftwaffe hurled 200 bombers against London in two waves, and such was the ferocity of the battle that at one stage – when the first wave attacked – the RAF had no more fighters in reserve. If more bombers had attacked immediately afterwards, the Spitfires and Hurricanes would have been on the ground and London would have taken fearful punishment. As it was, the second wave did not attack until two hours later, by which time the fighter squadrons

were once again ready for it. A total of 148 bombers got through to bomb the capital, but 56 were shot down and many more were severely damaged. One Dornier 17 pilot who got back reported that KG 3's airfield at Antwerp 'seemed to be littered with wrecks'. There were Dorniers with collapsed undercarriages, Dorniers with shattered cockpits, Dorniers with half their tails shot away. Ground crews stared with horrified eyes as bullet-riddled aircraft taxied in. Not until this moment had they begun to imagine the havoc wrought by Fighter Command across the Channel on this 'Black Sunday'.

Towards the end of September a thick bank of cloud crept in over the British Isles and Western Europe. With the spell of bad weather came a complete revision of Luftwaffe tactics. Gone were the large daylight formations; the lesson of 15 September had been well and truly learned. Instead, the new tactics called for penetration raids by small groups of aircraft in good weather, and interdictor missions by solitary bombers and fighter-bombers in all kinds of conditions.

On the morning of 20 September, twenty-two Messerschmitt 109s crossed the English coast at an altitude of 27,000 feet, then went into a long, shallow dive in the direction of London. At exactly 13,000 feet each pilot pressed a release, and twenty-two 500-lb bombs dropped away to explode in the City. After this attack, one-third of all available 109s were adapted to carry bombs, but after the initial surprise the RAF soon got the measure of the new tactics and the fighter-bombers began to suffer heavy losses. By the end of November the scheme had been abandoned altogether.

Meanwhile, having failed to achieve its objective during daylight, the Luftwaffe began to step up its night attacks on London. The Battle of Britain

The front page of the *Daily Mail*, 16 September 1940 (reproduced as image).

Daily Mail, Monday, September 16, 1940.

Daily Mail

FOR KING AND EMPIRE

LATE WAR NEWS SPECIAL

ONE EGG makes scrambled egg for two when the milk is mixed with a teaspoon of BROWN & POLSON CORNFLOUR

THE KEENEST BLADE CHADE

NO. 13,852   *   MONDAY, SEPTEMBER 16, 1940   ONE PENNY

175 (and more) DOWN

GREATEST DAY FOR RAF

Half Raiders Brought Down

26 FT. DOWN

They Battled with Ton Time-bomb

MORE than 175 German 'planes and at least 350 airmen were shot down in the morning and afternoon attacks on London yesterday.

The R.A.F. lost 30 machines and 10 airmen. In addition, German losses include:

18 on Saturday

Million Cheer London Battle

LONDON had its greatest thrill of the war yesterday when German bombers were shot down in daylight raids at Victoria, Kennington, and Streatham.

It was a day of mass raiding — and mass defeats.

350 CAME, ONLY 175 RETURNED

HITLER'S air force returned to mass daylight raids yesterday and the R.A.F. gave them the most shattering defeat they have ever known.

The Air Ministry state that between 350 and 400 enemy aircraft were launched in two waves against London and south-east England.

Of these no fewer than 175 were shot down, four of them by A.A. fire. This is a proportion of nearly one in two destroyed. All these are "certainties," for the total does not include "probables."

The R.A.F. lost 30 'planes, and ten of the pilots are safe.

Most of the raiders that were not destroyed were harassed all the way back to France.

A considerable section of Hitler's invasion fleet in the Channel ports have now been destroyed by the R.A.F.

On Saturday night our bombers gave the invasion ports their most severe battering to date.—See Back Page.

The ports of Antwerp, Ostend, Flushing, Dunkirk, Calais, and Boulogne were heavily bombed for seven

Another Hospital Bombed

PATIENTS SAFE

By Daily Mail Raid Reporter

GERMAN bombers, bound on their nightly terror raiding, arrived at 8.10 last evening.

London's terrific barrage of A.A. guns, stronger than ever at times, forced them to adopt new tactics.

Circling round London at leisure was no longer safe. Instead, flying at a great

THIS Daily Mail picture-diagram shows the task that faced the St. Paul's bomb squad. You can see the direction in which the bomb was slipping, 26ft. down, threatening the Cathedral more and more each moment.

PALACE

ST. PAUL'S IS SAVED BY SIX HEROES

By Daily Mail Reporter

A LITTLE party of experts—an officer, Lieut. R. Davies and five men—have saved St. Paul's Cathedral from almost certain destruction by a gigantic German time-bomb which fell from a 'plane on Thursday and buried itself 26ft. deep in a crater near the walls.

Yesterday at noon, after three days' continuous work, the bomb, 8ft. long, fitted with fuses which made it perilous to handle, was secured by steel tackle and hauled to the surface with a pulley and cable attached to two lorries.

It was one of the biggest that had fallen in London and weighed a ton.

A City fireman who had been on duty continuously in the area told me:

"There were five of them, all young fellows, officered by a French-Canadian. One was an Irishman and a couple came from Yorkshire. Another, I believe, came from Lancashire.

"On the first day they couldn't start work because a six-inch gas-main, broken by the bomb, was blazing. But they've been here from early morning till dusk ever since.

"It was wonderful to watch. They used no scaffolding or supports, and there was a risk of the road falling in at any moment.

"After digging through gravel and sand they came to black

Westminster Abbey Hit

The west window of Westminster Abbey was slightly damaged during a recent air-raid.

"The damage was very slight, and only a few small squares were broken," said an official.

The Clare Reported Missing

From Daily Mail Correspondent

NEW YORK, Sunday.—The British flying boat Clare is missing on her third flight from England to the United States, says the New York Daily News.

"Fear in aviation circles that the machine met with disaster is increased by a wireless message that a huge 'plane' was forced

LATEST

BERLIN ALARMS

Berlin, Monday.—An air-raid alarm was sounded in Berlin at 11.20 p.m. yesterday. The All Clear sounded at 11.35.

A second alarm was given at 1.55 a.m. to-day, the All Clear following at 2.10 a.m. Anti-aircraft fire was heard in the city.—B.U.P.

5 KILLED IN STREET

A London hospital was hit by an incendiary bomb during yesterday's raid.

---

had ended in victory for the RAF, but the ordeal of the cities was only just beginning.

On the night of 14 November 1940, 450 German bombers wiped out the heart of the lovely cathedral city of Coventry – classed as a legitimate military target because of its munitions factory – with 500 tons of high explosives and 30 tons of incendiaries. This raid marked the start of a new and terrible phase in air warfare – the era of mass night bombing. Night after night, during that desperate winter of 1940/41, the pattern was repeated. For three months London, the Midlands, Lancashire, South Wales, Tyneside, Plymouth, Exeter, Southampton, Bristol and many other places reeled under the avalanche of fire from the night sky. At this stage Britain's night-fighter defences were primitive. During the first year of the war British bombers shot down more aircraft at night than did the RAF fighters. Nevertheless, as the year drew to its close RAF fighter pilots began to report increasing success against the night raiders. A handful of men, often flying aircraft totally unsuited to night-fighting, began to specialize in stalking and destroying the enemy over the burning cities. One such was Flight Lieutenant Richard Payne Stevens.

On the night of 15 January 1941 thousands of Londoners must have looked up to see a long white vapour trail spearing across the sky, threading its way through a maze of twinkling shell-bursts. At the head of the trail was Stevens, flying a Hurricane of No. 253 Squadron. He had taken off from Manston half an hour earlier, at 12.56, as reports began to come in of enemy raiders heading for London. Now, at 15,000 feet, he could see the flashes of anti-

ABOVE The front page of the *Daily Mail*, 16 September 1940.

OPPOSITE Dornier 17s flying above fires started by bombs in the Royal Victoria Docks area of east London.

aircraft shells ahead of him; somewhere in that area of sky was an enemy bomber. Suddenly he saw it; the long, dark shape of a Dornier 17, fleeting across the stars in a steep turn. Slamming open the throttle, Stevens went after it. The Dornier went into a fast climb up to 30,000 feet and then levelled out. Stevens closed in to less than fifty yards, waiting until the black bulk filled his sights before pressing the firing-button. Debris bounced off the Hurricane and oil sprayed back on to the windscreen as the Dornier lurched and stalled. Stevens shoved the stick hard over, avoiding a collision by a hair's breadth. The bomber went into a dive and Stevens followed it down to 3000 feet, when it began to climb again. At that moment Stevens fired; the Dornier burst into flames and crashed into a wood.

Three hours later Stevens was airborne once again, looking down on London from 17,000 feet. He had almost given up his search and was on the point of turning for home when he sighted a Heinkel 111. He got on the bomber's tail and fired a long burst into it; the Heinkel went down and crashed in the Thames Estuary, two of the crew bailing out.

Later that year Stevens took the fight right into the enemy's camp. Flying a four-cannon Hurricane IIc fitted with long-range fuel tanks, he would take off from Manston and disappear eastwards into the gathering darkness. Patiently, he would loiter over the enemy's bomber airfields in France and Belgium, waiting his chance to shoot down the bombers on their own doorstep. Between January and December 1941 he destroyed fourteen enemy bombers at night. At 19.45 on 15 December 1941 he took off as usual on one of his freelance intruder missions. The hours of the night dragged by; at Manston his ground crew waited for the familiar sight of his black-painted Hurricane slanting down out of the eastern darkness. They waited long beyond the fighter's maximum endurance, but Flight Lieutenant R. P. Stevens never came back.

In the summer of 1940 the mainstay of the RAF's hastily organized night-fighter squadrons was the Blenheim IF, which was totally unsuited to night operations and which, for the most part, was slower than the bombers it was supposed to catch. Then, in August 1940, the RAF's night-fighter force received unexpected reinforcements in the shape of two squadrons, Nos. 141 and 264, equipped with Boulton-Paul Defiants. Unexpected, because the debut of the Defiant as a night-fighter came about more or less by accident as a result of the severe mauling the two squadrons received at the hands of the Luftwaffe during daylight operations. By the middle of August both Defiant squadrons were flying operationally at night, the first probable success being scored by No. 264 on the night of 15 August. No. 141's first real taste of night-fighting came during the second week of September, when the Luftwaffe stepped up its night attacks on London; on the night of the fifteenth/sixteenth 'B' Flight Defiants operating from Biggin Hill shot down two Heinkels. The squadron moved to Gravesend early in November to guard the approaches to London, while No. 264 operated north of the Thames from Rochford and later from Debden. During the following weeks more Defiant squadrons were formed; first of all No. 307 (Polish) Squadron, operating from Jurby in the Isle of Man with the task of defending Northern Ireland. It moved to Squires Gate for the defence of Merseyside early in 1941. By the spring of that year five more Defiant squadrons had been formed: Nos. 85, 96, 151, 255 and 256. Night after night, during the Luftwaffe's big air offensive against the British cities in the early part of 1941, they combed the night skies in search of enemy bombers, but claims were few.

OPPOSITE TOP The Supermarine Spitfire Mark II.

OPPOSITE BOTTOM A Bristol Beaufighter equipped with airborne interception radar. These long-range night-fighters were first issued to squadrons in September 1940.

It was left to the Beaufighter squadrons to write a new chapter in the story of night-fighting. The first Bristol Beaufighters began to reach the squadrons in September 1940, at the height of the Battle of Britain. Fast and heavy, the twin-engined aircraft was highly unpopular at first; in fact some pilots went as far as to call it a suicide machine. Wild rumours circulated about its performance. It got out of control easily in a tight turn; it stalled viciously; and the engines had a habit of failing at crucial moments. It was true that there was some initial trouble with the Beaufighter's engines, but this was rectified fairly quickly. It was also true that it was not a novice's aircraft; it was a thoroughbred and as such needed a masterful touch. But in the hands of a skilled pilot the Beaufighter, with its armament of four cannon and six machine-guns, was a formidable weapon. There was also another point in the Beaufighter's favour; it was the only aircraft big enough to carry the early, bulky Mk IV airborne interception radar without sacrificing other weight in fuel and fire-power.

The first squadrons to receive Beaufighters were No. 25 at North Weald, No. 29 at Digby, No. 219 at Catterick and No. 604 at Middle Wallop. On 8 September 1940 a fifth squadron, No. 600 at Hornchurch, also began to re-equip. The first confirmed kill went to No. 219 on the night of 25 October, when a Beaufighter flown by Sergeant Hodgkinson with Sergeant Benn as his observer shot down a Dornier 17. The first kill following a radar interception was scored by a No. 604 Squadron aircraft on the night of 19/20 November, when Flight Lieutenant John Cunningham – who was to become the RAF's leading night-fighter ace – and Sergeant J. Phillipson stalked and shot down a Junkers 88.

The night-fighters' score continued to mount steadily from January 1941, with the introduction of GCI – Ground Controlled Interception – stations along the south coast of England. From these stations the controllers were

able to bring the fighters within a mile or so of their target, at which point airborne radar took over to complete the interception. On the night of 15/16 April 1941 John Cunningham set up a new night-fighting record by destroying three enemy bombers in a single night with the assistance of GCI.

Three nights later, on 19/20 April, the Luftwaffe launched a 'maximum effort' night assault on London. A total of 712 bombers flew against the British capital, and 24 of them were shot down by night-fighters – the latters' biggest success so far. The raid marked the virtual end of the non-stop air offensive against Britain; ten days later the Luftwaffe began to withdraw their bomber units to the east in readiness for the assault on Russia. By 21 May only four out of the original forty-four bomber groups were left on the Channel coast.

7 Mediterranean Air War

On 11 June 1940 – the day after Italy's entry into the war on the side of Germany – a radar unit on the island of Malta reported an Italian air raid approaching from Sicily. Despite Malta's importance as a strategic bastion in the Mediterranean, the air defence of the island at this time consisted of only six Gloster Sea Gladiator fighter biplanes, two of which immediately took off to intercept. Before they could reach the Italians, however, the latter had dropped their bombs on Valetta docks and made their escape.

The bombers came back that afternoon, this time escorted by Fiat CR.42 and Macchi C.200 fighters, and once again the Gladiators failed to intercept. During the days that followed the Gladiator pilots were forced to develop new tactics to cope with their faster opponents; these involved climbing above the enemy formations before the latter reached Valetta and then diving through them, using the speed of their dive to make one quick firing pass and upset the Italians' bombing runs.

In the first ten days of the war with Italy the Italian Air Force made seven attacks on Malta, but the Gladiators failed to shoot down any enemy aircraft. The first victory came on 22 June, when a lone SM.79 reconnaissance aircraft appeared over the island. A Gladiator flown by Squadron Leader G. Burges was airborne, and managed to get into a good attack position before the Italian crew sighted it. The SM.79 crashed in the sea and the crew were taken prisoner.

The Gladiators shot down two more Italian aircraft that week, and on 28 June Malta's defences received a boost in the shape of four Hawker Hurricanes, flown in from North Africa. They came just in time, for only two Gladiators were now airworthy. More Hurricanes arrived on the aircraft carrier HMS *Argus* early in August, and a complete Hurricane squadron – No. 261 – was soon fully operational on the island.

The Italians launched a new series of attacks in November 1940. Several enemy aircraft were shot down by No. 261's Hurricanes and the Italians changed their tactics, sending small numbers of fighter-bombers over the island on hit-and-run raids. No. 261 countered these by mounting standing patrols over Malta, with a flight of Hurricanes patrolling at high level and the two surviving Gladiators lower down.

By the end of 1940 Malta had developed into a vital offensive base, with island-based RAF bomber squadrons attacking enemy targets in Italy, Sicily and North Africa. Then, in December, came a new development: the German Luftwaffe entered the battle, with the Stukas, Junkers 88s and Messerschmitts of Fliegerkorps X occupying Sicilian airfields in strength.

On 11 January 1941 the Luftwaffe began a massive air onslaught against Malta. It continued almost without pause through the first three months of the year, during which period the Hurricanes of 261 Squadron and half a dozen Fleet Air Arm fighters remained the island's sole air defence. The fury of the attacks abated somewhat after March 1941, although they never

ceased entirely. Meanwhile, the build-up of RAF aircraft on the island continued, and by October three Hurricane squadrons were based there.

Throughout the summer months of 1941 the Malta-based bomber squadrons had been striking hard at German and Italian shipping in the Mediterranean, and the losses they inflicted were so severe that the Luftwaffe High Command decided to make a final all-out attempt to destroy the island's air capability. For this purpose the Germans assembled 250 bombers and 200 fighters on airfields in Sicily and southern Italy; against this armada the RAF could muster a mere 60 Hurricanes.

The renewed German air offensive began a few days before Christmas 1941, with waves of bombers attacking Malta's airfields between the rainstorms that lashed the area at this time of the year, and by the second week of

ABOVE LEFT *SS Talbot*, bombed by enemy planes, burns in the Grand Harbour at Malta.

ABOVE RIGHT One of the three Gloster Gladiators stationed in Malta.

January only Luqa was still serviceable. As a direct result of these attacks the volume of supply traffic crossing the Mediterranean to replenish the enemy forces in North Africa showed a marked increase, and with German bombers inflicting substantial losses on Allied supply convoys to Malta, the island's position was fast becoming critical.

In March 1942 Malta's air defences were reinforced by the arrival of fifteen Spitfires, ferried in at enormous risk by the aircraft carrier HMS *Eagle*; they arrived at a time when only thirty serviceable Hurricanes were left. In April, while these aircraft continued the fight, the determined stand of the island fortress was honoured by the award of the George Cross.

On 20 April forty-seven more Spitfires arrived on Malta after flying from the aircraft carrier USS *Wasp*; their arrival, however, had been detected by the Germans, and within hours their airfields were under attack by large formations of enemy bombers. By the end of the next day, after further heavy raids, only eighteen of the original forty-seven Spitfires were still in an airworthy condition. On 9 May the USS *Wasp* returned, together with HMS *Eagle*, and between them the carriers flew off sixty-four more Spitfires, which were thrown into action almost immediately. The following day saw a major air battle over the island when the Luftwaffe made a determined effort to sink the minelayer HMS *Welshman*, which had docked in Valetta harbour laden with supplies and ammunition. Between them the island's Spitfires and Hurricanes flew 124 sorties that day, destroying fifteen enemy aircraft. Three Spitfires were lost, but two of the pilots were picked up by the air-sea rescue service.

Seventeen more Spitfires arrived later in May and deliveries of fighter aircraft continued throughout the summer months of 1942; HMS *Eagle* alone delivered 182 Spitfires before she was sunk by a U-boat on 11 July. Most of the ferry work was subsequently undertaken by HMS *Furious*, which flew off thirty-seven Spitfires on the day HMS *Eagle* went down, followed by twenty-seven more on 7 August. Several RAF pilots distinguished themselves during the summer months of 1942; one of them was the Canadian-born Pilot Officer George F. Buerling, who scored twenty-seven victories

ABOVE AND LEFT Bristol
Beaufighters in Malta.

BELOW AND BOTTOM Bristol
Beaufort bomber, torpedo and
reconnaissance aircraft.

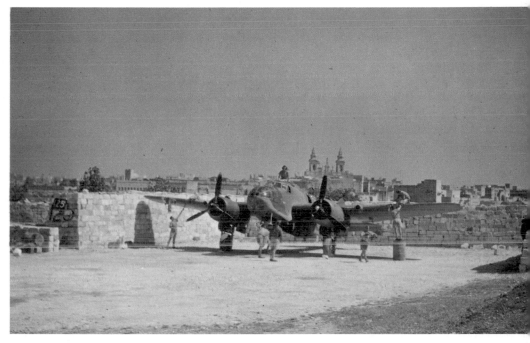

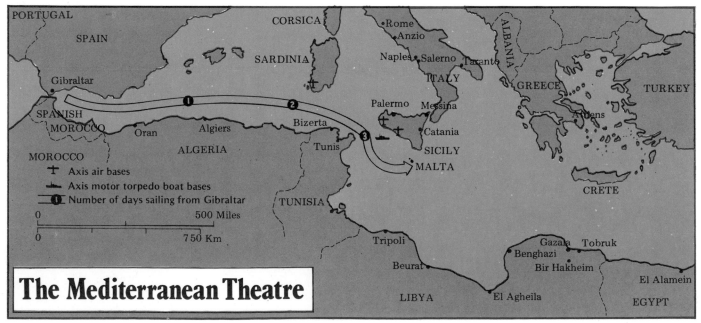

The Mediterranean Theatre

OPPOSITE An Italian Fiat CR.42.

LEFT A Hawker Hurricane Mark I on patrol over the desert.

while flying Spitfires over the island. He survived the war only to be killed while ferrying an aircraft to Israel in 1948.

The enemy air raids continued, reaching their climax in November 1942 when the Germans subjected Malta to a furious round-the-clock bombardment that lasted ten days. The defenders remained unbroken, and the offensive against the supply convoys ferrying desperately needed reinforcements to the German forces in North Africa went on almost unchecked. The battle for Malta was over; by the end of the year most of the Luftwaffe units in Sicily had been withdrawn for service on other fronts. In the early months of 1943 Malta was turned into a vast aircraft carrier and supply base as the Allies built up their resources for the offensive that would take them across the narrow straits to Sicily and, ultimately, to the Italian mainland.

While the RAF and the Luftwaffe battled in the skies of Malta, the air war had raged no less furiously in other sectors of the Mediterranean theatre. Considerable success had been achieved right at the start of the war with Italy by three squadrons of RAF Gladiator fighters, which saw action over the Egyptian border against the Italian Air Force in June and July 1940; No. 33 Squadron, for example, shot down thirty-eight enemy aircraft and destroyed twenty more on the ground in six weeks of combat, while the Gladiators of No. 80 Squadron destroyed nine Italian Fiat CR.42 fighters in a single day for the loss of only one of their own machines.

Not long afterwards these two squadrons and the third Gladiator unit in Egypt, No. 112 Squadron, were sent to Greece, which had been invaded by the Italians. No. 80 was the first to arrive and was detailed to support the Greek Army fighting hard on the Albanian frontier; its pilots had shot down forty enemy aircraft by the end of the year, when they were joined by their colleagues of No. 112 Squadron. In January 1941, when the Gladiators of No. 33 Squadron also arrived in Greece, bad weather hampered air operations, but on 9 February fourteen Gladiators of No. 80, led by Flight Lieutenant M. T. St J. Pattle, encountered a formation of forty Fiat G.50 fighters and shot four of them down for no loss. Pattle, a South African, was credited with the destruction of thirty enemy aircraft – and possibly more – during operations in Egypt and Greece; he was shot down and killed on 20 April 1941 while commanding No. 33 Squadron.

By the end of February 1941 all three RAF fighter squadrons in Greece were re-equipping with Hurricanes, and these operated side by side with the remaining Gladiators. On 28 February sixteen Hurricanes and twelve Gladiators were patrolling at 14,000 feet when they sighted a formation of fifty Italian bombers and fighters. While the Gladiators circled round the enemy formation to cut off its escape, the Hurricanes attacked it furiously. In the ensuing air battle the RAF fighters claimed no fewer than twenty-seven aircraft destroyed – all of which were confirmed by observers on the ground – and a further eleven probably destroyed.

The success, however, was destined to be short-lived, for in April the Germans entered the battle for Greece. By 19 April concentrated attacks by the Luftwaffe on the Greek airfields had reduced the strength of the RAF fighter squadrons to only twenty-two serviceable aircraft, and a few days later all but seven of the Hurricanes were destroyed in low-level strafing attacks by Messerschmitts. With this blow, Allied air resistance over Greece virtually ceased to exist.

On 1 May the last Commonwealth forces were evacuated from the Greek mainland, and 30,000 Allied troops worked desperately to prepare the island of Crete to meet an enemy invasion. The island's entire air defence force consisted of 14 fighters; against them were ranged 430 enemy bombers, 180 fighters, 700 transport aircraft and 80 assault gliders. During the first two weeks of May German dive-bombers carried out a furious air bombardment of Crete, with the island's three airfields as their main objectives, and by the nineteenth only four Hurricanes and three Gladiators were still airworthy. The next day this pitiful remnant was withdrawn to Egypt, and the Germans were now free to launch their airborne invasion. In a desperate, last-ditch attempt to re-establish a fighter defence the RAF sent six Hurricanes back to Crete, but two were shot down by friendly anti-aircraft fire as they approached the island and the others were destroyed in bombing attacks soon after their arrival. By the end of May the battle of Crete was over, with about half the island's defenders killed or captured.

In March 1941, while the Allies still fought desperately in Greece, the German Afrika Korps arrived in Libya under the command of General Erwin Rommel, and the British forces were soon in retreat along the road they had taken in their victorious advance against the Italians a few months earlier. The British garrison at Tobruk was completely surrounded, and to provide fighter cover the Hurricanes of Nos. 6 and 73 Squadrons were flown in. With their airstrip under continual shellfire, operational conditions were grim, and by 25 April No. 73 Squadron was so depleted that it had to be withdrawn, leaving the Hurricanes of No. 6 as the only operational aircraft within the Tobruk perimeter. They, too, had to be withdrawn on 10 May.

Meanwhile new Allied squadrons were being hurriedly formed to challenge the Luftwaffe's air superiority, and in the spring of 1941 the RAF in the Western Desert was joined by Commonwealth units from Australia and South Africa. The build-up of the Desert Air Force continued throughout the summer months, in readiness for 'Operation Crusader' – the plan to relieve the Tobruk garrison – and by November there were forty fighter squadrons in the Middle East, equipped primarily with Hurricanes and American-built Curtiss P-40 Kittyhawks.

'Operation Crusader' began on 18 November, with the British Eighth Army thrusting towards Tobruk. The troops were supported by the Allied fighter and fighter-bomber squadrons, which carried out constant attacks on Rommel's armoured divisions. The Afrika Korps fought hard for a week before Rommel broke off the engagement and withdrew to the west, still hammered by the Desert Air Force, and the Germans now worked hard to establish a defensive line based on Gazala. This line was broken in December by a new Eighth Army offensive and the Allied forces pushed on towards Benghazi, but they were halted at El Agheila.

OPPOSITE TOP Curtiss Kittyhawks of No. 112 Squadron in the Western Desert.

OPPOSITE BOTTOM Supermarine Spitfire Mark Vs, fitted with tropical filters, in the Western Desert.

RIGHT A tanker and trailer on fire
after receiving a direct hit from a
Bristol Blenheim on a desert road.

In January 1942 Rommel counter-attacked in strength; the Allied air
effort was severely hampered by flooding on the forward airstrips, and for
the first forty-eight hours the fighter-bombers were able to give only limited
support to the Eighth Army. Emergency strips were quickly laid and the
Hurricane and Kittyhawk squadrons concentrated on these, carrying out
non-stop ground attack operations and re-establishing air superiority over
the battlefield.

The Germans, nevertheless, were able to continue their advance, and by
February they had pushed the Eighth Army back as far as Rommel's former
defensive line between Gazala and Bir Hakheim. This line held firm until
May, when three German divisions outflanked Bir Hakheim and cut off the
1st Free French Brigade. The French gallantly resisted every enemy assault
for ten days and the Desert Air Force threw every fighter it could spare into
the battle. The Hurricanes and Kittyhawks wrought great execution among
the formations of Junkers 87 dive-bombers which were battering the fortress,
and No. 6 Squadron – now flying Hurricane IIds armed with 40-mm cannon
– struck hard at the encircling enemy armour and artillery. By 10 June, however, the position of the French Brigade was hopeless, and the survivors were
ordered to fight their way out. By pinning down the German divisions the
French had bought time for the Eighth Army to regroup and withdraw
into Egypt.

In August 1942 General Montgomery assumed command of the Eighth

Army, which was then holding a short defensive line in western Egypt from El Alamein to the Qattara Depression. On 31 August Rommel attacked the El Alamein position in full strength, but the Eighth Army held on grimly and inflicted heavy losses on the enemy, while the Desert Air Force continued to increase its overall superiority. By this time the Hurricanes and Kittyhawks which had borne the brunt of Allied fighter operations for so long were being reinforced by more modern combat types, including Spitfires and Beaufighters. No. 145 Squadron was the first to receive Spitfires in the desert, in June 1942; it was joined later by Nos. 92 and 601 Squadrons.

One of the first German fighter units to arrive in Africa back in April 1941 had been Jagdgeschwader 27, whose Messerschmitt 109s had been in almost continuous action ever since. Among JG 27's officers was a twenty-one-year-old fighter pilot whose name had become legendary on both sides of the front: Jochen Marseille, who flew a Messerschmitt 109 with a distinctive yellow '14' painted on its fuselage. In eighteen months of operations Marseille claimed the destruction of no fewer than 158 Allied aircraft, often shooting down several in a single day. His claims were bitterly disputed by the Allies, and yet all were verified by Marseille's fellow pilots or German ground forces.

Marseille attributed his success to his ability to retain full control of his fighter while manœuvring at low speed, which usually enabled him to turn inside his opponent. He was also an excellent deflection shot. On 5 June 1942, when he landed after shooting down six Kittyhawks of No. 5 Squadron, South African Air Force, his astonished armourers discovered that he had used only ten 20-mm shells and 180 rounds of machine-gun ammunition.

No British fighter pilot ever brought Marseille to account. On 30 September 1942, while returning to base after an uneventful escort mission, his Messerschmitt caught fire without warning and he baled out. His horrified comrades saw his body strike the tailplane and plummet to earth like a stone. They buried him where he fell, amid the sand and scrub of the desert.

By 5 September 1942 it was clear that Rommel's offensive – hampered by continual air attack on his overstretched supply lines – had failed, and the Eighth Army prepared a massive counter-attack at El Alamein. This unfolded on 23 October 1942 and the entire strength of the Desert Air Force's fighter-bomber squadrons was turned on the reeling enemy, who finally broke on 4 November. The coastal roads leading to the west were jammed with enemy convoys, which were harried mercilessly by the fighter-bombers during the pursuit into Cyrenaica.

Meanwhile the Allies had launched 'Operation Torch': a massive landing on the coasts of French Morocco and Algeria by seaborne British and American forces. Caught between the two Allied pincers, the Germans sought to establish new defences in Tunisia and seized a number of ports, through which they attempted to pour in supplies. In April 1943 the Eighth Army linked up with the US II Corps and the final advance through Tunisia began, with the fighter-bomber units in the forefront of the battle all the way. On occasions RAF Hurricane squadrons actually operated from temporary landing-grounds behind the enemy lines, attacking the Germans from the rear.

By May the Afrika Korps was tottering to defeat. In a desperate, last-ditch attempt to provide reinforcements, huge convoys of Junkers 52 and Messerschmitt 323 transport aircraft left Italy and Sicily for the German-held

RIGHT Douglas Bostons over desert terrain.

Tunisian airfields; they were caught by formations of Allied fighters, often while still far out to sea, and slaughtered. On 18 April, for example, forty-seven P-40 Warhawks of the US Ninth Air Force, together with twelve Spitfires of No. 92 Squadron, RAF, intercepted a formation of ninety Junkers 52s escorted by fifty German and Italian fighters and destroyed seventy-seven of them for the loss of six Warhawks and one Spitfire. This great air battle, which went down in history as the 'Palm Sunday Massacre', resulted in the destruction of more enemy aircraft than the RAF shot down in one day at the height of the Battle of Britain. On 22 April RAF Spitfires followed up this success by shooting down twenty-one massive

Messerschmitt 323 six-engined transports, all heavily laden with troops.
It was the end. On 13 May 1943 the remnants of the Afrika Korps finally surrendered. They had fought valiantly to the last, tumbling from the height of victory to crushing defeat; a defeat brought about in no small measure by the Desert Air Force and the RAF squadrons on Malta, which had battled through fearful odds to win overwhelming air superiority for the Allied cause in North Africa.

ABOVE The cockpit of a Douglas Boston.

8 Air War on the Eastern Front, 1941-45

At first light on 22 June 1941, 120 German divisions launched 'Operation Barbarossa' – Hitler's invasion of the Soviet Union. Following the classic tactics used during the Battle of France a year earlier, the attack was spearheaded by panzer divisions and an overwhelming concentration of air power – nearly 800 bombers and 480 fighters.

During that first morning of the campaign in the east, the Soviet Air Force in the western sector was decimated as the Luftwaffe pounded one air-base after another. On one airfield alone, German fighter pilots found nearly a hundred Russian aircraft lined up in neat rows; for twenty minutes the Messerschmitts roved back and forth, reducing the base to a burning shambles. Nevertheless, despite the almost total surprise achieved by the Germans some Russian squadrons took to the air and fought the invaders desperately; several Soviet fighter pilots deliberately rammed their opponents. The air fighting was not all one-sided; although the Messerschmitts were faster than both standard Russian fighter types, the I-16 and I-153, the German pilots found themselves outmanœuvred time and again. The Russian pilots fought on the turn and the Germans often found it impossible to keep the enemy in their sights. When a Russian pilot found himself in a difficult spot he would simply haul his aircraft round in a tight turn and race head-on for the nearest Messerschmitt at full throttle. These tactics usually worked, unnerving the German pilots and forcing them to break away sharply.

Courage, however, was not enough. By noon on 22 June, 800 Russian aircraft had been destroyed. By nightfall this figure had risen to 1,489, including 322 shot down by flak and fighters. The Luftwaffe's losses during the day's fighting amounted to a mere thirty-five aircraft. On the last day of the month the Russians threw every available bomber into action in an attempt to stem the German flood; they were unescorted and the Luftwaffe shot them down in scores. Jagdgeschwader 51, operating in the Minsk sector in support of Panzer Group 2, destroyed 114 enemy aircraft on 30 June alone, while further north over the Dvina River the Messerschmitts of JG 54 accounted for 65 more.

Day after day the slaughter went on. Luftwaffe fighter pilots who had arrived on the Eastern Front with no combat experience found themselves turned into aces almost overnight as Russian aircraft went down before their guns. Yet the apparent suicide of the Soviet Air Force was serving a purpose: at the cost of thousands of aircraft and lives, the Russians were buying time. Aircraft factories in the west were dismantled and reassembled in Siberia, beyond the range of the Luftwaffe's bombers, and although this massive evacuation caused a temporary drop in the monthly production total of military aircraft by 50 per cent the figure had risen to 1000 machines a month by the spring of 1942.

During the summer of 1941 Russian fighter-production concentrated on

The Eastern Front

LEFT Yakovlev Yak-1 fighters on the production line.

TOP The I-16 fighter.
ABOVE A MiG-1 fighter.

the more modern types that had already begun to replace the elderly I-16s and I-153s in service: the Yak-1, MiG-1 and LaGG-3. These machines equipped the squadrons that took part in the defence of Moscow, which was subjected to a series of very heavy air raids during the summer and autumn, and six Russian fighter units that particularly distinguished themselves in the battle were designated Guards Regiments. As the war progressed, these and subsequent Guards Regiments became the Red Air Force's elite backbone, their ranks numbering Russia's best fighter pilots.

In January 1942 the Russians – encouraged by their successful defence of Moscow, and with their front-line forces bolstered by fresh combat divisions from Siberia – launched a major offensive on the Kalinin Front against the German Army Group Centre. Compared with the effort it would be called upon to make in the future, the Soviet Air Force's contribution to this offensive was small – but it was significant. For the first time Soviet air units

showed themselves capable of holding their own against the Luftwaffe, and on the Moscow and Rostov Fronts the Russian fighter pilots even established a measure of air superiority. Their success was due in no small measure to the robust nature of their aircraft and equipment, which were better suited to the fearful operating conditions of the worst Russian winter in living memory. For most of the winter months the majority of Luftwaffe units were forced to operate with fewer than half their available aircraft.

With the spring thaw, however, the Germans regained the initiative by launching a massive offensive in the Crimea, with 74 divisions supported by 1500 aircraft. Further north a second German offensive in the Donets Basin practically wiped out five Russian field armies, which were trapped and encircled by the speeding panzer divisions. The stage was now set for the great push that was designed to take the Germans through the eastern Ukraine to the Volga, for which they assembled a force of ninety divisions. In June 1942 the Germany Army Group B broke through the Bryansk Front and drove on towards the important strategic town of Voronezh, on the River Don, and through this breach the Sixth Army under General von Paulus struck southward, forcing the Russian armies into a retreat across the steppe. Ahead of the Germans, drawing them like a magnet, lay the Volga and the city of Stalingrad.

In August 1942, as the Sixth Army forged on towards its goal, Stalingrad became the target for a massive air onslaught by the Luftwaffe. On the twenty-third, as the first German spearheads reached the Volga, 200 German bombers escorted by 50 Messerschmitts attacked the city. They were intercepted by the Yak-3 fighters of the Russian 102nd Air Division, which was responsible for the defence of Stalingrad, and a fierce battle raged across the sky. During that day the Soviet fighter pilots over Stalingrad and the surrounding front claimed the destruction of ninety German aircraft for the loss of thirty of their own.

A number of Soviet pilots joined the ranks of the air aces by destroying five or more enemy aircraft during the battle for Stalingrad. One of the leading pilots was Mikhail Baranov, who went on to score twenty-eight

ABOVE Petlyakov Pe-2 light bombers.

RIGHT Alexander Pokryshkin, Russia's second-ranking ace of the Second World War, with his MiG-3 fighter.

victories. On one occasion, while leading a section of four Airacobras – American fighters supplied to the Russians – he encountered twenty-five Messerschmitts over Stalingrad and shot down three of them; then, his ammunition exhausted, he chopped off the tail of a fourth with his propeller, afterwards making a forced landing.

Another Russian pilot to achieve fame over Stalingrad was a woman: Lieutenant Olga Yamshchikova of the 586th Fighter Regiment, an all-female unit. She became the first woman pilot to destroy an enemy aircraft at night when she shot down a Junkers 88 over the embattled city on 24 September 1942. The 586th Regiment subsequently fought its way across Europe in the wake of the Soviet Army, finishing the war in Austria. By that time its female pilots had flown a total of 4400 operational missions and destroyed forty enemy aircraft in combat.

As the battle for Stalingrad wore on, new Russian fighter types began to appear at the front. The first was the Lavochkin La-5, a development of the earlier LaGG-3 which proved to be 30 mph faster than the Messerschmitt 109. The other was the Yakovlev Yak-9, a highly manœuvrable little fighter destined to become, to the Red Air Force, what the Spitfire was to the RAF. Many Russian fighter regiments re-equipped with either the La-5 or the Yak-9 during the winter of 1942/43.

In January 1943, as the Russian ring of steel closed relentlessly round the trapped German Sixth Army in the Stalingrad pocket, the Soviet Army launched a major offensive against the Germans on the Kuban Peninsula, where the Wehrmacht had been building up large forces in readiness for a drive into the Caucasus. During the Kuban battle, when large formations of Russian and German aircraft clashed over the front line, the Russians developed new fighter tactics which were to remain standard in the Red Air Force throughout the rest of the war. The best-known of all Russian air fighting exponents was Guards Major Alexander Pokryshkin, whose formula for successful air combat was simple: 'Altitude – Speed – Manœuvre – Fire!' Altitude meant that a fighter pilot always had the initiative, enabling him to select his target and get into a good attacking position, while speed meant that he could close rapidly on an adversary with less danger of being attacked from the rear himself. Using these tactics, Pokryshkin shot down three enemy aircraft in one sortie over the Kuban. His Yak-9 fighter, with a large white '100' painted on its side, soon became famous on both sides of the front. He was to end the war with fifty-nine confirmed victories, making him the second top-scoring Russian pilot.

The summer of 1943 found the Soviet central front in a precarious position, with two German salients at Orel and Kharkov flanking a deep bulge to the west of Kursk. If the Germans could break the Russian defences north and south of Kursk, they would succeed in trapping and destroying the vast Russian forces in the salient. It would be a disaster from which the Red Army would have little hope of recovering. For their planned offensive the Germans had assembled nearly a million men in seventy divisions, supported by large numbers of tanks and 1700 aircraft. Several Luftwaffe fighter squadrons were now equipped with the redoubtable Focke-Wulf 190, and the German pilots had high hopes of establishing clear air superiority over the battlefield.

When the German offensive opened on 5 July 1943, however, it was the Red Air Force that struck the first blow. At dawn 400 Russian fighters and bombers swept over the front line towards the enemy-held airfields around Kharkov, where most of the Luftwaffe's squadrons were concentrated. The Russians were intercepted by the Messerschmitts and Focke-Wulfs of Jagdgeschwader 3 and 52, and a tremendous air battle – the biggest of the whole war, with at least 500 aircraft involved – spread out over the sky. The Russian attack was broken up and the German fighters claimed the destruction of seventy enemy aircraft for the loss of twenty of their own number. Only a few of the Russian bombers succeeded in getting through to the German airfields, and they inflicted little damage.

This first day of battle saw both sides throw their air power on a massive scale against tanks and infantry. Much devastation was wrought by the Red Air Force's ground-attack squadrons, equipped for the most part with Ilyushin Il-2 Sturmovik assault aircraft armed with 37-mm cannon. On one occasion a formation of these aircraft wiped out seventy German tanks of the 9th Panzer Division in the space of twenty minutes. On the second day Russian fighters once again appeared over the front in strength and more fierce dogfights flared up over the Kursk salient, with heavy losses on both sides.

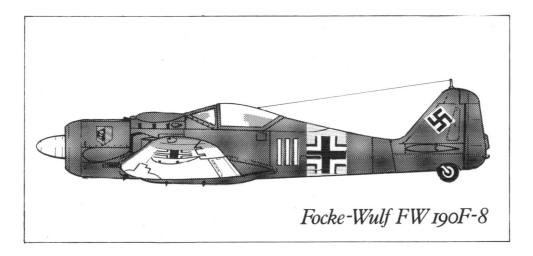

Focke-Wulf FW 190F-8

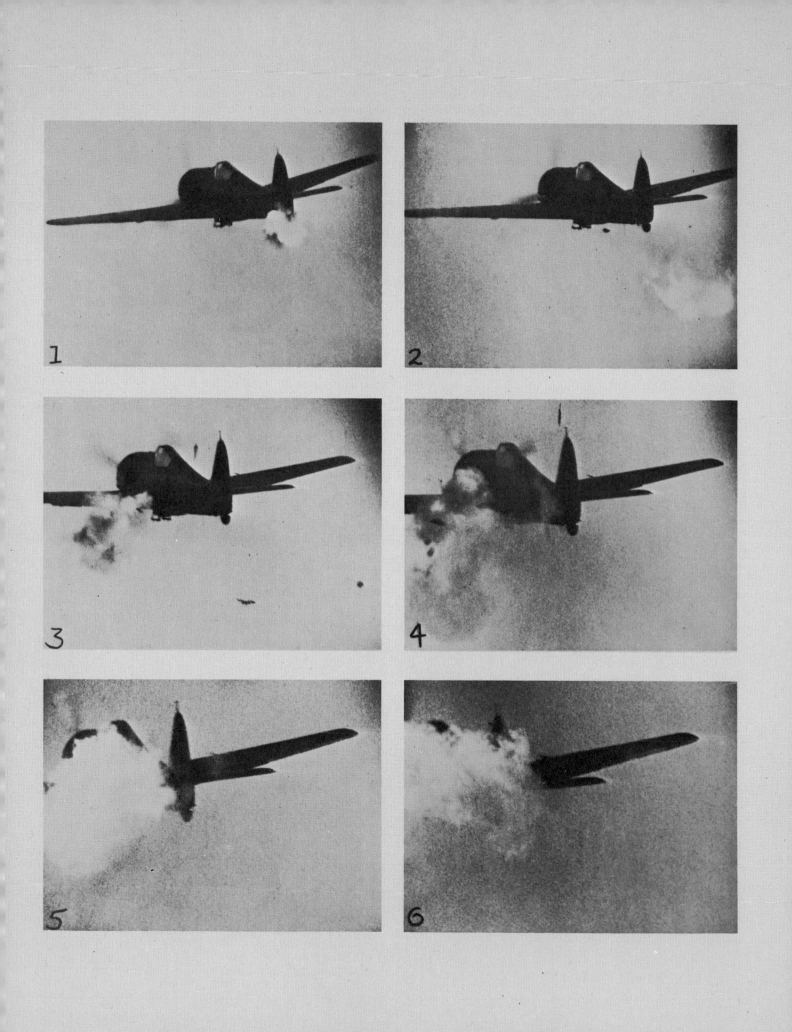

On this day a young Russian second lieutenant named Ivan Kozhedub scored his first victory: a Junkers 87 Stuka. The next morning he shot down another Stuka, followed by a pair of Messerschmitts the day after. He had opened a score that was to end in the sky of Berlin twenty months later with sixty-two enemy aircraft destroyed, making him Russia's top-ranking air ace. Kozhedub was only one of the Russian fighter pilots who had their baptism of fire over Kursk; another was Guards Lieutenant A. K. Gorovetz, who destroyed no fewer than nine Stukas in a single engagement during the battle.

For a Russian pilot to register such a high score in the course of one air fight was unusual, although a number of Luftwaffe fighter pilots managed to amass a near-incredible total of 'kills' while fighting on the Eastern Front, often claiming the destruction of nine or ten enemy machines in one day – especially during the early months of the campaign, when the Red Air Force was fighting at a disadvantage in every respect. Leading the Luftwaffe scoreboard was Lieutenant Erich Hartmann, who served with Jagdgeschwader 52 on the Russian Front from the autumn of 1942 and who went on to claim an incredible 352 victories. Several other German pilots claimed a score that ran into three figures, and although these totals were later bitterly disputed, it should be remembered that the staggering number of kills achieved by the Luftwaffe on the Eastern Front were made possible by two principal factors: the inexperience of the rank and file of their opponents, and the fact that many German pilots served almost continuously in action against the Russians for nearly four years, with only short leave breaks. The overall result was that as the skill of individual fighter pilots grew, the Russian Front became the 'happy hunting-ground' of air fighting. The Russians themselves held the top German fighter pilots in considerable awe; they dubbed Erich Hartmann 'Cherniye Chort', or 'Black Devil', and offered a reward of 10,000 roubles to anyone who shot him down. Hartmann, in fact, survived the war only to be handed over to the Russians. He spent ten years in a prison camp before his eventual return to Germany.

There is no doubt that Kursk was the decisive battle of the Eastern Front. Within eight days the German offensive had been broken and the Russians had begun a series of strong counter-attacks, exploiting their success all along the line. In August 1943, supported by 100 air divisions totalling 10,000 aircraft, the whole Soviet battlefront began to roll forward in a relentless drive that would not cease until it reached the heart of Germany. In three weeks the Russians recaptured Orel, Belgorod and Kharkov, and in September they established a bridgehead on the Dnieper in readiness for an assault on Kiev. This city was taken after bitter fighting in November, before the grip of winter brought a halt to further major offensive action.

By the beginning of 1944 the Soviet Air Force had established definite air superiority, and although the Luftwaffe was still a force to be reckoned with the calibre of its aircrews was beginning to show a marked decline. Russian equipment, moreover, was at long last a match for anything the Germans possessed, and fighter operations were now closely co-ordinated. By the end of 1943 the Red Air Force was operating its first radar equipment, which the Soviet industry had just begun to manufacture; its operational use was pioneered by the fighter regiment commanded by Alexander Pokryshkin on the Crimean Front in January 1944.

In March 1944 Soviet forces under Marshal Koniev set foot on Rumanian soil, and in an effort to dislodge them the Germans launched a strong

OPPOSITE Six split second stages in the disintegration of a Focke-Wulf 190.

ABOVE The La-7 fighter in which Ivan Kozhedub, three times Hero of the Soviet Union, finished the war.

counter-offensive at Yassy. To provide air cover the Luftwaffe had assembled some of its finest fighter squadrons, opposed on the Russian side by a number of Guards Fighter Regiments. As these units met in combat, the battle of Yassy was marked by air fighting of a savagery unmatched since Kursk, with the Luftwaffe hurling wave after wave of fighter-bombers against the Soviet ground forces.

It was the last time that the Luftwaffe made a serious attempt to gain air superiority over the battlefield on the Eastern Front, and it ended in failure. The Russian fighters enjoyed overwhelming numerical superiority, and Luftwaffe losses were high. After Yassy the German squadrons were shared out piecemeal along the front, and although the pilots still fought gallantly their operations lacked cohesion. There were few of the Luftwaffe's elite left now; many had survived three years of bitter fighting in the east only to give their lives in a hopeless attempt to stem the Allied air onslaught from the west. A few of the men who replaced them were of high calibre, but most were overwhelmed before they had a chance to prove their worth.

In April 1944 the Red Army liberated the whole of the Crimea. This was followed by a major offensive on the Byelorussian Front, which was to end with the encirclement and annihilation of thirty German divisions in the Minsk sector. By mid-July the German Army Group Centre had virtually ceased to exist and the Russians were spearing into Poland.

At the end of the year the Eastern Front ran from Yugoslavia to the Baltic,

Lavochkin La-7

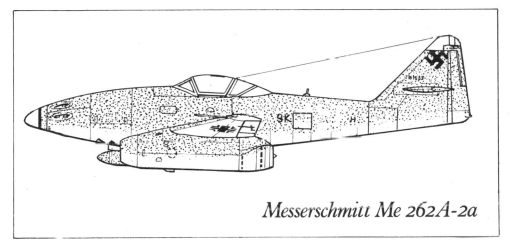

Messerschmitt Me 262A-2a

slicing across Poland and Czechoslovakia and running along the border of East Prussia. The stage was now set for the great Russian offensive that would take them deep into Germany. For this last mighty thrust they had assembled five million men, and to support it there would be a vast air umbrella of thirteen air armies totalling 17,000 aircraft, outnumbering the dwindling Luftwaffe squadrons by ten to one.

In this last phase of the battle the Germans had organized no fewer than eight lines of defence, and the Russian armies suffered staggering losses as they assaulted them one by one. Over the battlefield massive formations of Soviet fighters operated in three zones, covering the whole front. The forward zone, inside enemy territory, was patrolled by the Guards Fighter Regiments and other crack units, their task being to intercept and break up any enemy formations before they reached the battle area itself. Dislocated, the enemy units would then fall prey to other powerful fighter groups patrolling the second and third zones, the latter being directly over the front line.

In April 1945 the Russians stood poised on the Oder and Neisse Rivers, where the Germans had created their main line of defence. Despite crippling losses, the Luftwaffe continued to throw its dwindling reserves of combat aircraft into the fray, including Messerschmitt 262 jets; three of these were shot down by Russian fighter pilots, one of whom was Ivan Kozhedub.

The Russian armies on the Oder-Neisse front were supported by 8400 combat aircraft, and at dawn on 16 April 1945 these launched an all-out

ABOVE Ilyushin Il-2 Sturmoviks over Berlin.

attack on the German positions west of the line. In its wake the Russians launched their offensive, and within a week – after savage fighting and appalling cost – they had succeeded in smashing the German Ninth Army. Then, on 21 April, came the news that the crack Soviet Eighth Guards Army under General Chuikov – the veteran defender of Stalingrad – was fighting in the suburbs of Berlin itself.

As the Russian advance rolled forward, the supporting air units operated from stretches of autobahn. The time involved in repairing these was far less than it would have taken to build new forward airstrips, and the woods that ran along either side of the roads provided excellent camouflage for dispersed aircraft. For some time now, the Luftwaffe had also been operating combat aircraft from this ready-made network of emergency runways.

From these forward strips the Soviet fighter formations roved across the sky of the burning German capital. The Luftwaffe went on fighting hard to the last, the German pilots hurling themselves against the great Russian armada with suicidal courage. Scraping together their last reserves, they flew an average of a thousand sorties a day during the month-long battle for Berlin. It was a drop in the ocean; in one day alone, during the final assault on the capital, the Soviet air armies flew nearly 17,000 missions.

On 2 May, pounded incessantly from both air and ground, the last defenders of Berlin surrendered. There remained only a few isolated pockets of resistance in the east; the last was Prague, which held out for a week after the fall of Berlin. On 9 May, the day of the final German surrender in Prague, Major V. Golubev – one of Pokryshkin's pilots, and sixteenth-ranking Soviet air ace – shot down a Messerschmitt 109 over the city. It was the last aircraft to be destroyed in air combat during the European war.

118

9 The Battle of Germany

During the grim days of 1940 and 1941, with one European territory after another falling to Hitler's victorious Wehrmacht, Great Britain had only one means of bringing the war home to the people of Germany: the growing power of RAF Bomber Command. Compared with the mighty Anglo-American strategic bombing offensive that was to unfold later in the war, these early efforts were pinpricks; the crews of the Wellingtons, Whitleys and Hampdens that were the mainstay of Bomber Command up to 1942 had to battle their way across darkened Europe with little in the way of navigational aids, and only a small percentage of the bombs dropped actually fell in the target areas.

In 1942, however, the squadrons of Bomber Command were re-equipping with three new types of four-engined bomber, the Avro Lancaster, Handley Page Halifax and Short Stirling, and at last Germany's cities and industries began to feel the weight of the British night offensive. In May and June 1942 the RAF launched three thousand-bomber attacks against Cologne, Essen and Bremen, causing substantial damage, and the ability of Bomber Command to hit its targets in massive strength began to give rise to serious concern in Luftwaffe circles that the German air defences were seriously deficient in many respects.

By the end of 1942 German fighter production stood at 600 aircraft per month, and this figure would be doubled by the middle of the following year. It was still not enough. As fast as the fighters were being produced they were being swallowed up by the front-line squadrons in Russia, western Europe and the Mediterranean; the defence of the Reich still took second place. And for Germany the martyrdom was only just beginning; for in 1943 she would be the target of a mighty combined British and American air onslaught whose aim was, in the words of the directive that unleashed it, 'the progressive destruction and dislocation of the German military, industrial and economic system and the undermining of the morale of the German people to a point where their capacity for armed resistance is fatally weakened'.

In the summer of 1942 the first bomber squadrons of the United States Eighth Air Force had become operational on British bases, and during the remainder of the year they had carried out many daylight attacks with strong fighter escort against targets in France and the Low Countries. Attacks on targets further afield presented problems, for the Allied fighters did not have sufficient range to escort the bombers all the way. Nevertheless, the preliminary attacks on 'fringe' targets in Europe had been encouraging enough to persuade the Americans that the risk was justifiable – despite the warnings of the RAF, who had bitter experience of the cost of unescorted daylight missions over enemy territory.

The first daylight mission over Germany undertaken by the Americans, a raid on Wilhelmshaven by a relatively small number of B-17 Flying Fortresses in January 1943, was almost unopposed and seemed to bear out their belief that the heavily armed bombers, flying in tight 'boxes', could bring enough defensive fire-power to bear to deter most enemy fighter attacks. Before many weeks had elapsed, however, determined packs of Luftwaffe fighters had shattered this myth once and for all, although it took them some time and losses before they discovered the Fortress's vulnerable spot – a head-on frontal attack, followed by a half-roll and dive beneath the bomber formation.

The Eighth Air Force's raids continued to grow in size – and cost. As the Germans' experience of countering the heavy bombers increased, American losses rose to a serious level during April and May 1943; but the real test was still to come. In June 1943 the RAF and USAAF joined forces in 'Operation Pointblank', a round-the-clock bombing offensive against Germany's war industries. In terms of offensive power the Eighth Air Force was well equipped to undertake such an operation; by the beginning of July its strength had increased to fifteen bomber groups. The biggest obstacle to the success of deep-penetration daylight missions still remained the lack of long-range fighter escort; in an effort to fill this critical gap the Americans slung drop-tanks under the wings and bellies of their P-47 Thunderbolt and P-38 Lightning fighters, which enabled them to penetrate as far as Germany's western frontier, but this did not provide a real solution. It was not long before the German fighter leaders developed new combat techniques that went a long way towards eliminating the Americans' advantage; the Fokke-Wulfs and Messerschmitts would attack the US fighters as they crossed the Dutch coast, forcing them to jettison their auxiliary tanks in order to increase manœuvrability.

During the last week of July 1943 the Eighth Air Force carried out five major attacks on enemy targets; eighty-eight bombers failed to return. This loss would undoubtedly have been much higher had it not been for the escort

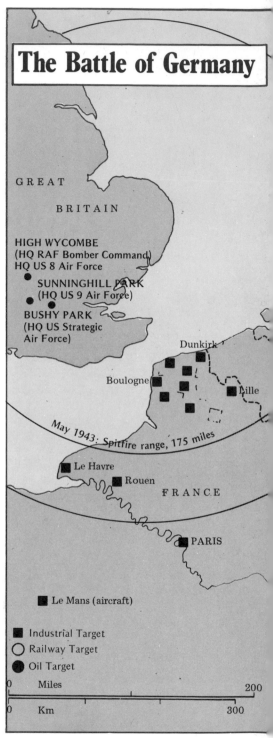

The Battle of Germany

GREAT

BRITAIN

HIGH WYCOMBE
(HQ RAF Bomber Command)
HQ US 8 Air Force
● SUNNINGHILL PARK
(HQ US 9 Air Force)
BUSHY PARK
(HQ US Strategic
Air Force)

Dunkirk

Boulogne

Lille

May 1943: Spitfire range, 175 miles

Le Havre

Rouen

FRANCE

PARIS

■ Le Mans (aircraft)

■ Industrial Target
○ Railway Target
● Oil Target

0   Miles   200

0   Km   300

LEFT A Handley Page Halifax of RAF Bomber Command during a daylight raid in the Ruhr.

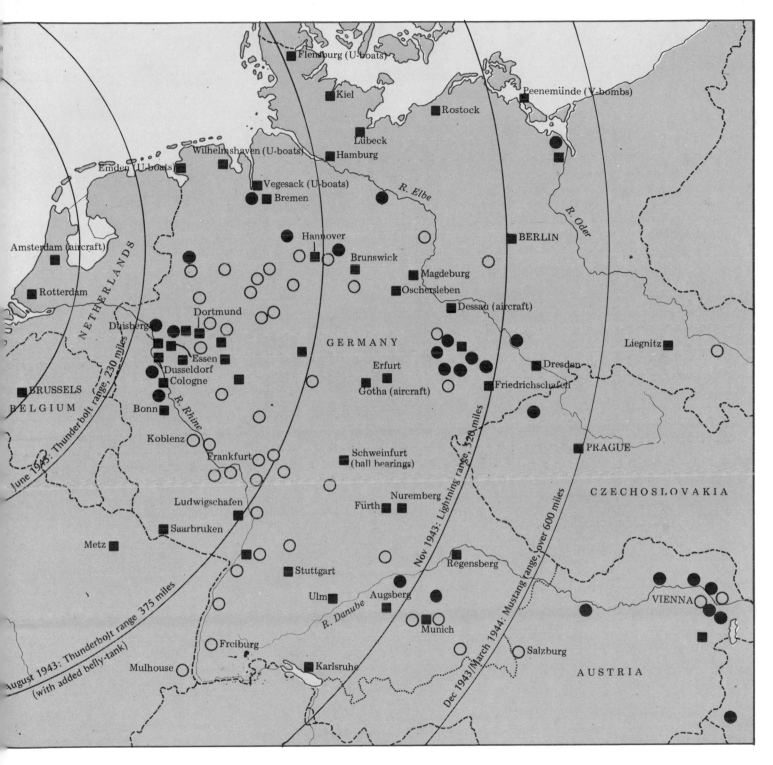

of P-47s and P-38s with long-range tanks. Then came August, and the first of a series of shattering blows for the Americans. On the seventeenth an armada of B-17 Flying Fortresses and B-24 Liberators attacked the Messerschmitt factories at Regensburg and the ball-bearing plant at Schweinfurt; they encountered determined German fighter attacks as soon as they entered enemy territory, and the fury did not diminish. The enemy fighter groups attacked in pairs, one engaging the American fighter escort and the other the bombers. At times more than three hundred German

fighters were in the air, and fierce battles raged all along the route. In addition to cannon and machine-guns, some of the fighters were armed with 21-cm rockets; salvoes of these dislocated several bomber formations, and the fighters then pounced on individual aircraft. On this grim day the Americans lost sixty bombers, with a hundred more damaged; it would be five weeks before they recovered sufficiently from this mauling to carry out further long-range missions over Germany.

When the attacks did start again, the lessons of August were rammed home even more forcibly. During one week between 8 and 14 October the Americans lost 148 bombers and 1500 aircrew. In an attack on Schweinfurt on 14 October the Luftwaffe fighters made 500 sorties and destroyed 60 of the 280 bombers taking part – more than 20 per cent.

Developments in German night-fighting techniques were also beginning to inflict heavy losses on RAF Bomber Command. Three major raids on Berlin in August and September 1943 cost the RAF 123 Lancasters and Halifaxes, with a further 114 damaged. Many of these losses were due to new German tactics known as '*Wilde Sau*' (Wild Boar), in which the pilots of formations of single-engined fighters patrolled over the German cities and picked out the British bombers in the glare of searchlights and fires. With the introduction of more advanced airborne interception radar, the German night-fighters – mainly Messerschmitt 110s, Junkers 88s and Dornier 217s – presented a serious challenge to Bomber Command, and their success rate reached its peak in the spring of 1944. In the course of three major battles over Germany the RAF suffered crippling losses; the worst was on the night of 30 March, when Bomber Command lost ninety-five heavy bombers over Nuremberg, with a further seventy-one damaged.

TOP Handley Page Halifax bombers.

ABOVE Dornier Do 217 medium bombers in formation.

OPPOSITE TOP The deservedly famous Avro Lancaster bomber.

OPPOSITE BOTTOM Bombing-up a Short Stirling.

123

As the Americans reeled under the losses sustained during the daylight offensive of 1943, it was clear that only one thing could redress the balance in their favour: a suitable long-range fighter. By the end of the year they had it in the shape of the North American P-51 Mustang, which flew its first operational mission from Britain with the 354th Fighter Group in December. On the thirteenth of that month it escorted B-17s to Kiel and back, a round trip of a thousand miles. More long-range escort missions were flown in January and February 1944 and the results were encouraging, the Mustangs claiming the destruction of over fifty enemy fighters.

Even so, one Mustang Group was not enough to bring about a dramatic reduction in the losses suffered by the heavy bombers, and early in 1944 these once again reached alarming proportions. On 11 January, for example, 60 out of 238 bombers that attacked aircraft factories at Oschersleben failed to return. The following month there was another tragedy when 430

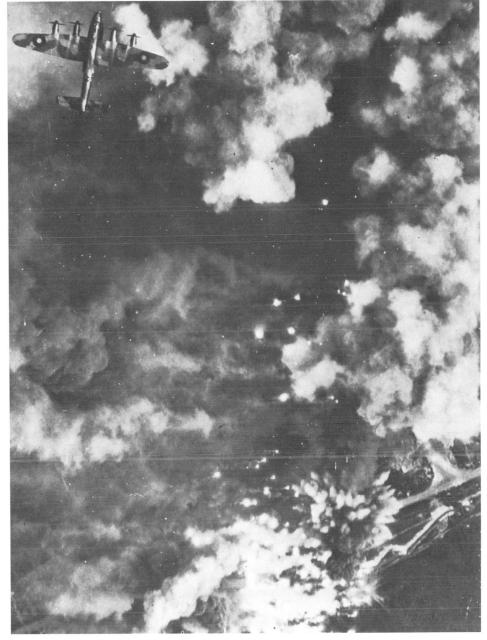

ABOVE LEFT Flying Fortresses of the 8th USAAF wing across the sky on a raid against German installations.

ABOVE RIGHT An RAF Avro Lancaster over its target.

OVERLEAF Three Short Stirling bombers.

North American P-51B-15 Mustang

RIGHT The damaged tail and rear
turret of a Short Stirling after a raid
on Duisburg during April 1943.

bombers set out to bomb factories in central Germany; shoals of German
fighters attacked them before they rendezvoused with their Mustang escort,
and 44 Fortresses and Liberators were shot down.

The tables, however, were beginning to turn. On 6 March 1944, Mustangs
appeared for the first time in the sky over Berlin and took part in one of the
most bitterly contested air battles of the war. For hours a raging battle was
fought between 200 German fighters and 660 heavy bombers and their
escort. When it ended the Americans had lost 69 bombers and 11 fighters,
but the Germans lost 80 aircraft – almost half the defensive force.

As more Mustang groups entered the battle during March, the German
air defences became noticeably weaker. Day after day in that fateful spring
and early summer of 1944 the solid phalanxes of bombers dragged their
contrails over the shattered cities of the Third Reich, selecting their targets
almost at will. The dwindling band of Luftwaffe fighter pilots fought them
with desperate courage, but against the swarms of Mustangs and Thunderbolts courage was not enough. The Luftwaffe was sliding rapidly towards a
crushing defeat; a defeat inflicted not by the bombing of its resources on the
ground, but by the daily struggle against murderous odds high above the earth.

The Luftwaffe's only solution to this appalling rate of attrition was to mass-produce a fighter superior to any in service with the Allies – a fighter that would enable the Germans to regain air superiority over their homeland. Such an aircraft – the Messerschmitt 262 jet – already existed, but its entry into service had been subjected to innumerable delays, not the least of which was Hitler's insistence that the type should be converted for use as a 'reprisal bomber'. Had large numbers of 262s been available during the critical summer months of 1944, when the Allies launched their long-awaited invasion of Europe, the outcome of the war might have been very different. As it was, the 262 was not mass-produced as a fighter until November 1944, and it was not until January 1945 that the first units were fully operational.

The Allies began to feel the full impact of the enemy jet fighters in March 1945. On the eighteenth, when 1250 American bombers set out for Berlin to deliver the heaviest attack of the war on the German capital, their formations were intercepted by thirty-seven Me.262s of Jagdgeschwader 7, which shot down nineteen bombers for the loss of two of their own number. Most of the bombers were destroyed by R4M air-to-air rockets, twenty-four of which were carried by each 262 on underwing rails. On 4 April the 262s of JG 7 repeated their success by shooting down fifteen B-17s over Nordhausen, and four days later the jet fighters demonstrated their enormous speed advantage over piston-engined types by shooting down twenty-eight Mustangs, Lightnings and Thunderbolts in air battles that raged across north and central Germany.

Nevertheless, there was no escaping the fact that on this same day no fewer than 133 piston-engined Messerschmitt 109s and Focke-Wulf 190s were destroyed by Allied fighters. No matter how many successes were scored by the German jets, they were too few and it was too late; the Allies remained firmly in control of the air.

On the tactical side, too, the Luftwaffe was decisively beaten; the Allied tactical air forces had achieved superiority during the Normandy landings, and they never relinquished it during the months that followed. The Luftwaffe made only one serious attempt to deal a decisive blow to the Allied air forces; it happened on 1 January 1945, at the height of the German counter-offensive in the Ardennes – the operation known as the 'Battle of the Bulge'. On New Year's Day, 1000 low-flying German bombers and fighter-bombers struck twenty-seven Allied airfields in Belgium and Holland, destroying nearly 300 British and American aircraft on the ground in the space of a few minutes. The raid, which cost the Luftwaffe about 140 aircraft, virtually paralysed the tactical air force for over a week, during which time the Allied air effort was sustained almost entirely by a single RAF Fighter Wing: No. 122, equipped with Hawker Tempest fighters.

It was not long, however, before the Allies were operating at full strength again; the Luftwaffe had played its last card, and it had lost. During the weeks that followed the Mustangs, Thunderbolts, Lightnings, Spitfires and Tempests roved across Germany, ferreting out the dwindling Luftwaffe squadrons and attacking them on their airfields. Fighter-bombers also struck hard at enemy communications in northern Germany in preparation for 'Operation Varsity', the Allied crossing of the Rhine. This took place on 24 March 1945; the fighters of the Second Tactical Air Force successfully prevented the Luftwaffe from interfering, and in fact only a few enemy aircraft were sighted. German flak, however, was intense, and seventy-five Allied aircraft were shot down.

OPPOSITE TOP Boeing B-17 Flying Fortress formations in flight.

OPPOSITE BOTTOM The de Havilland Mosquito, one of the most versatile aircraft of the Second World War. It was the fastest light bomber of the war, a distinguished long-range day and night fighter and unequalled for photo-reconnaissance.

ABOVE Avro Lancaster bombers.

RIGHT The Hawker Typhoon, one of the best ground-attack aircraft of the Second World War.

ABOVE Boeing B-17 Flying
Fortresses over target.

With the Anglo–American forces firmly established across the Rhine
and the Russian armies closing in from the east, the collapse of German
resistance was rapid. The Luftwaffe continued to operate from its remaining
airfields and stretches of autobahn, but the fierce, courageous pilots who had
challenged the RAF in the early days of the war had perished in the great
killing-ground of the sky over western Europe, and those who replaced them
were no match for the experienced Allied airmen. But they were brave; they
fought on to the end, despite the hopelessness of their situation.

On 30 April 1945, as rocket-firing Hawker Typhoons of the RAF and
Thunderbolts of the USAAF harried the last Tiger tanks among the
shattered streets of Germany's towns and villages, fifty Focke-Wulf 190s and
Messerschmitt 109s made a courageous attempt to attack the advancing
troops of the British Second Army. The Spitfires and Tempests pounced,
and after a bitter dogfight the debris of thirty-seven enemy aircraft lay
scattered over the countryside.

That same day Adolf Hitler killed himself beneath the ruins of Berlin, and
a week later the war in Europe came to an end.

10 Pacific Air War

As the bitter year of 1941 drew to a close the Allies began to see the first faint glimmer of hope in their struggle against Germany. In North Africa General Erwin Rommel's forces had suffered their first reverse at the hands of the British Eighth Army, while in Russia the German offensive had ground to a halt at the gates of Moscow.

Then, on 7 December, came the first of a series of shattering blows which, in the weeks to come, would alter the whole basis of Allied strategy: the Japanese attack on Pearl Harbor in the Hawaiian Islands, devastating the American Pacific Fleet and paving the way for further conquests. By the end of December the Japanese had invaded Thailand, Burma and Malaya, had captured Wake Island and Hong Kong, and had carried out a major landing on Luzon, in the Philippines. These early conquests were a triumph of air power, and particularly naval air power; and it was naval aviation that would be the dominant factor in the great battles that were to come. The one significant failure of the Japanese strike on Pearl Harbor was that it had not destroyed the US Pacific Fleet's three aircraft carriers, which had been at sea at the time; these now formed the nucleus of the US Navy's first carrier task force, the forerunner of a mighty weapon that would ultimately carry the war back across the Pacific to the Japanese home islands.

The overwhelming superiority of Japanese naval air power came as a complete shock to the Allies, and the nastiest surprise of all was the enemy's ability to provide strong fighter escort for their bombers over incredible distances. The fact was that for several months before the Pearl Harbor attack Japanese Navy pilots had been working hard to develop low-speed cruising tactics that almost doubled the radius of action of their fighters. On 8 December 1941, for example, forty-five Mitsubishi Zero fighters – the Japanese Navy's standard type – escorted a formation of bombers from Formosa to carry out an attack on the Philippines, a round trip of 1200 miles.

The A6M Zero fighter soon showed itself to be clearly superior to any fighter the Allies could put into the air in the early stages of the Pacific War. Armed with two 20-mm cannon and two machine-guns, it was highly manoeuvrable and structurally very strong. Its main drawback was that it had no armour-plating for the pilot and no self-sealing fuel tanks, which meant that it could not absorb as much battle damage as Allied fighters. One well-placed burst of gunfire was usually enough to make the Zero explode in mid-air – and for the pilot that meant certain death, for the Japanese carried no parachutes.

During the first months of the Pacific War the Zeros carved out an impressive combat record. In the battle for Java, which ended on 8 March 1942, they destroyed 550 Allied aircraft, including large numbers of fighters such as the Brewster Buffalo, Curtiss CW.21, Curtiss Hawk, Curtiss P-40 and Hawker Hurricane. Japanese losses were extremely light. In one big dogfight that took place over Surabaya on 19 February 1942, twenty-three

LEFT The wreckage of American
aircraft at Pearl Harbor, after the
Japanese attack, 7 December 1941.

ABOVE A burned-out B-17C Flying
Fortress at Pearl Harbor after the
Japanese attack.

135

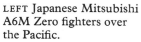

LEFT Japanese Mitsubishi
A6M Zero fighters over
the Pacific.

Mitsubishi A6M2 (Zero)

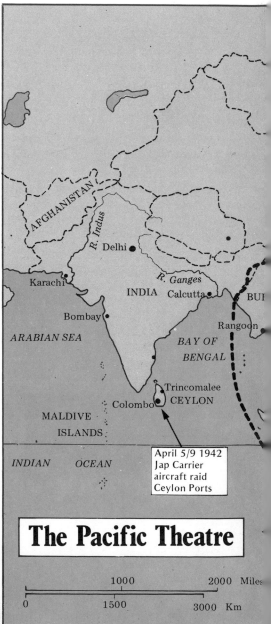

April 5/9 1942
Jap Carrier
aircraft raid
Ceylon Ports

The Pacific Theatre

Zeros operating from Borneo took on a force of fifty Dutch and American
P-36 and P-40 fighters and destroyed more than half of them for the loss of
only three of their own number.

These remarkable victories earned enormous prestige for the Japanese
Navy pilots and tended to overshadow the achievements of their Army
colleagues, who fought no less tenaciously albeit with less spectacular success. Throughout the war the demands of the Navy were to receive priority.

Unlike the Army, the Japanese Navy followed the practice of concentrating
its best pilots in elite units. One of these was based at Lae in New Guinea
in April 1942, and was assigned the task of providing fighter cover for the
Japanese drive towards Port Moresby. By the end of the month the Lae
Fighter Wing included such redoubtable pilots as Saburo Sakai, with 22
victories, Hiroyoshi Nishizawa with 13, and Takatsuka with 9. On 17

May, in a gesture of supreme defiance that symbolized their complete air superiority, Sakai, Nishizawa and another pilot named Ota carried out a series of aerobatics over the Allied air base at Moresby without being molested.

Most of the pilots of the Lae Wing continued to fly the Zero throughout their combat careers. Nishizawa, before being shot down and killed on 26 October 1944, was credited with more than a hundred victories; he destroyed six in a single day over Guadalcanal in August 1942. Another Japanese pilot, Kenzi Okabe, shot down seven American machines in one day over Rabaul. Saburo Sakai went on to end the war with sixty-two victories, making him the surviving Japanese top-scorer.

The Zero retained its overall ascendancy during the first two years of the Pacific conflict, even though the Japanese suffered some serious reverses during this period. The first of these was the Battle of the Coral Sea in May

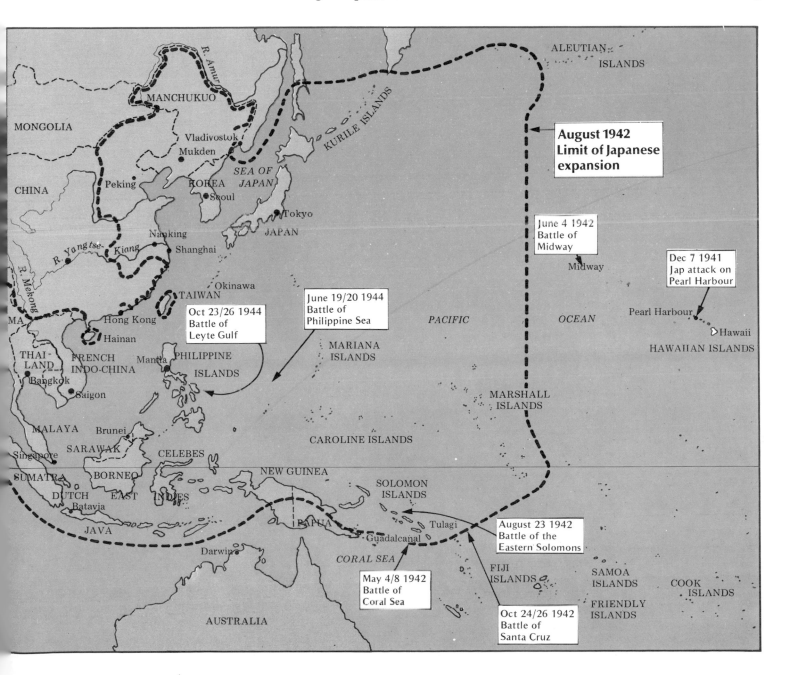

1942, when – in the first naval engagement of history fought without
opposing ships making contact – American carrier forces prevented the
Japanese from carrying out their proposed landing at Port Moresby, even
though American losses were higher than those of their adversary. Then, in
June, came the Battle of Midway, when United States carrier aircraft broke
up a strong enemy invasion force, sinking two heavy and two light carriers
and one heavy cruiser, and destroying 258 aircraft. This battle, in which the
Americans lost 132 aircraft and the carrier USS *Yorktown*, marked a definite
turning-point in the Pacific War. Not only did it bring an end to Japan's
offensive; it also resulted in the loss of a major part of the enemy's carrier
attack force and many of the Japanese Navy's most experienced pilots.

The standard American carrier-based fighter during the first months of
the Pacific War was the Grumman F4F-3 Wildcat, a type that was inferior
to the Zero on almost every count. Although very robust and capable of
withstanding a tremendous amount of battle damage, it needed a highly
experienced pilot at the controls to give the Wildcat a fighting chance of
survival in combat with the Japanese fighters. Nevertheless, a number of US
Navy pilots scored several noteworthy victories while flying the Wildcat;
on 20 February 1942, for example, while flying from the carrier USS
Lexington, Lieutenant Edward H. O'Hare destroyed five Japanese bombers
over Rabaul, while Lieutenant J. G. McCuskey of the USS *Yorktown* also
destroyed five during the Coral Sea battle. Another notable Wildcat pilot

Grumman F6F-3 Hellcat

was Captain Joe Foss, a Marine officer who went on to shoot down twenty-six enemy aircraft.

As the American pilots gained combat experience during 1942, their superior tactics and team-work began to have a telling effect on the course of the Pacific air war. Moreover, while the Japanese still relied on the fighter types with which they had begun the war – the Zero in the case of the Navy, and the Nakajima Ki-43 Hayabusa in the case of the Army – the United States aircraft industry was beginning to produce new combat aircraft which, before long, would enable them to wrest air superiority from the enemy. Taking note of the lessons learned in action by the Wildcat squadrons, the Grumman Aircraft Company designed a larger and more powerful version, the F6F Hellcat, which entered service in 1943 and which at last gave the US Navy pilots a chance to meet the Zeros on more than equal terms. Before the war ended, the Hellcat squadrons would be officially credited with the destruction of nearly five thousand enemy aircraft, or 80 per cent of all the kills scored by American carrier pilots during the Second World War.

Another new American type that entered the Pacific theatre in 1943 was the twin-engined, twin-tailed Lockheed P-38 Lightning, a long-range machine that substantially increased the radius that could be covered by land-based American fighter squadrons. One of the most famous of all operations carried out by the Lightning took place on 18 April 1943, when P-38s of the 339th Squadron, USAAF, shot down a Japanese bomber carrying Admiral Isoroku Yamamoto, the Japanese Navy C.-in-C. To do the job, the Lightnings made a 1100-mile round trip from Guadalcanal to intercept Yamamoto's aircraft over Kahili atoll. The two top-scoring American pilots of the Pacific War – Major Richard I. Bong and Major Tommy McGuire – both flew P-38s; Bong ended the war with a score of 40 enemy machines destroyed, while McGuire shot down 38 before his death in action over the Philippines in January 1945.

Early in 1943 some US Navy squadrons began to re-equip with a powerful new carrier-borne fighter, the Vought F4U Corsair. One pilot in particular scored spectacular successes while flying this type; he was Lieutenant Bob Hanson, a member of Marine Squadron VMF-215, and he rose to fame in the embattled sky over Rabaul. On 14 January 1944 Hanson fought the first of a series of combats that were to set a record, destroying five out of a formation of seventy Zeros that were trying to intercept American bombers.

His next five sorties over Rabaul netted him 1 Zero, 3 Zeros, 4 Zeros, 3 Zeros and 4 Zeros, which brought his score to 20 enemy aircraft destroyed over a period of only seventeen days.

From the spring of 1943 onwards American pilots began to notice a marked decline in the standard of their opponents; the loss of the nucleus of the Japanese Navy's best pilots, many of whom had seen extensive combat in China before the start of the Pacific War, in the great battles of 1942 was at last beginning to have its effect. As new American fighter types arrived in the Pacific, the Japanese began to suffer combat losses that were little short of staggering, and the US pilots – now skilfully led by veterans with two years of bitter experience behind them – gradually turned the whole combat theatre into a kind of happy hunting-ground, scoring formidable successes in dogfights that were often unbelievably one-sided.

In April 1943, for example, four P-38 Lightnings were carrying out a fighter sweep over Guadalcanal at 31,000 feet when they sighted three Zeros a thousand feet lower down. The P-38s dived to the attack and shot all three Zeros down in quick succession. Climbing again, the American pilots sighted a formation of Zeros attacking some US Navy Wildcats at 28,000 feet. The Lightnings burst through the middle of the fight at high speed in a shallow dive, knocking down two Zeros as they went. The Japanese broke in all directions and took evasive action, but two more Zeros went down in flames. In less than twenty minutes the four P-38s had accounted for seven of the enemy; none of the American fighters was damaged.

BELOW The twin-engined, twin-tailed Lockheed P-38 Lightning long-range fighter, introduced in the Pacific theatre in 1943.

ABOVE A Japanese Zero fighter
attempts a kamikaze attack on
USS *Missouri* during the Okinawa
campaign, April 1945.

OPPOSITE Aircraft and aft flightdeck
burn on a US carrier after a
kamikaze attack during the battle of
Leyte Gulf.

Even the Curtiss P-40 Tomahawk, a type which had suffered heavily at the hands of the Zeros in the early days of the war, was now capable of scoring overwhelming victories as superior American tactics, leadership and teamwork decided the outcome of air battles. This was superbly demonstrated one day in January 1944, when sixteen USAAF P-40s encountered thirty-six Japanese fighters and dive bombers off Saidor, New Guinea. The P-40s ripped through the enemy formation and three Japanese aircraft went down in flames. The remainder scattered, and in the ensuing dogfight the Japanese lost eighteen fighters and one dive-bomber. The P-40s suffered no loss. The American pilots observed that although the Japanese pilots were aggressive enough and eager to fight at the beginning, they quickly lost cohesion and threw caution to the winds in their efforts to escape.

In another major air battle of 1944 the Japanese lost 114 aircraft to the guns of the US Navy's Hellcats; the Americans lost only nine fighters. It happened on 24 June, during a long-range fighter sweep against the island of Iwo Jima. During the first mission of the day forty-eight Grumman Hellcats encountered more than a hundred enemy fighters over Iwo and destroyed thirty-three of them in the course of just a few minutes. Japanese torpedo aircraft tried to break through to the US task-force cruising off the island, but more Hellcats were waiting for them and they were massacred. One US fighter squadron, VF-2 from the carrier USS *Hornet*, destroyed sixty-seven enemy machines in the course of the day – a record for a Navy unit. By the end of the day, Iwo Jima's fighter defences had been annihilated and the island lay naked. The tragedy was that the Americans did not attempt an invasion until the following year, by which time the Japanese had poured troops and equipment into Iwo's defence.

Although the fighter squadrons of the Japanese Army and Navy received a substantial number of new combat aircraft during the last two years of the war, they never presented a serious challenge to Allied air superiority. One of the new types to enter service with the Japanese Army during 1943 was the Nakajima Ki-44 Shoki (Demon), known to the Allies by the code-name of 'Tojo'; it equipped many home defence squadrons and also served in Burma, Sumatra and New Guinea. One Shoki unit, the 87th Fighter Squadron of the Imperial Japanese Army Air Force, had the task of defending the vital oil refineries at Palembang in Sumatra, from which the Japanese obtained a large percentage of their aviation fuel.

On 24 January 1944 a British carrier task-force under Admiral Sir Philip Vian, on its way from Ceylon to join the American fleet in the Pacific, struck hard at the refineries with fifty Grumman Avenger bombers escorted by eighty Corsair and Hellcat fighters. They devastated the target and inflicted heavy losses on the enemy air defences. Major Hideaki Inayama, flying a Shoki fighter with the 87th Squadron, later described part of the air battle – and his account reveals how hard it was for the Japanese fighters to gain any kind of advantage over their determined opponents.

I climbed steadily to 9000 feet, performing lazy turns over the burning refineries. My forward visibility was now partly obscured by oil splashes on my windscreen, but I recognized two Shoki fighters flying some 3000 feet below me at ten o'clock. As I descended towards them I spotted the second attacking wave to the south. There appeared to be about 100 aircraft, with Avengers forming the bottom step of the wave at about 6000 feet ... The top cover of Hellcats broke formation, spreading into small combat groups. Keeping a wary eye on them, I headed for the Avengers, barrel-rolling up beneath them, loosing a burst at the nearest machine and climbing through their formation. Four escorting Hellcats were immediately on me and I turned sharply to port, two of the Hellcats overshooting.

The Shoki was fast and had an excellent rate of climb, but it was no match for the excellent little Grumman in manœuvrability. I pulled maximum 'g' which forced me down in the cockpit. The blood rushed to my head and I nearly blacked out. Glancing over my shoulder I saw that the nearest of my pursuers was 400 yards away. I flung my Shoki in a vertical turn to port. The leading Hellcat opened fire, but he could not bring his guns to bear effectively on my wildly turning fighter. I knew that my minutes were numbered, and then the unexpected happened. A burst of anti-aircraft fire landed slap in the middle of the Hellcats and they immediately broke to starboard ... I started to climb again, but the air battle seemed to be over.

The most devastating loss suffered in the air by the Japanese during the entire Pacific War occurred during the Battle of the Philippine Sea in June 1944, when carrier-based aircraft of the American Task Force 58 under Admiral Mitscher provided air cover for the occupation of the Marianas. During the first major fighter sweep over the islands, on 11 June, the carrier aircraft destroyed one-third of the defending air force. On the nineteenth, with the amphibious invasion in full swing, large numbers of Japanese bombers and torpedo bombers made a series of desperate attempts to hit the Task Force; they were detected by radar at a range of 150 miles, and the carrier fighters were waiting for them.

OPPOSITE A Japanese aircraft plunges into the sea after an unsuccessful attack on the stern of the American carrier USS *Kitkun Bay*, at the beginning of the Great Marianas Turkey Shoot.

ABOVE A Boeing B-29 Superfortress heavy bomber over Formosa.

RIGHT A comrade tightens a kamikaze pilot's *hachimaki*, a Samurai symbol of courage worn by all suicide pilots.

The great air battle that followed was a one-sided massacre that would go down in history as 'The Great Marianas Turkey Shoot'. The agile Hellcats swarmed all over the attackers before they even sighted the carriers; of the 200 Japanese aircraft in the first two strike waves, only 30 escaped. At the close of the day, the Japanese had lost a staggering 402 aircraft.

The capture of the Marianas was of great significance in the Pacific air war, for the islands provided the USAAF with a springboard to launch a long-awaited strategic air offensive against the Japanese home islands. At Saipan, Tinian and Guam work went ahead on the construction of new airfields, and by January 1945 these were ready to receive the strategic bombers: the mighty B-29 Superfortresses of the US Twentieth Air Force.

The first major B-29 attacks on Japanese targets, when the large-scale use of incendiaries caused fearful destruction, revealed the painful inadequacy of the Japanese air defences. The small night-fighter force was severely handicapped by the lack of advanced airborne interception radar. The standard Japanese night-fighter of 1945 was the twin-engined Kawasaki Ki-45 Toryu, known to the Allies by the code-name of 'Nick'; armed with one 37-mm and two 20-mm cannon, together with a 7.92-mm machine-gun, it would have been a formidable opponent if it had been equipped with anything but the most primitive AI radar. As it was, the day and night defence of Japan came to be borne increasingly by single-engined day-fighter types, and in the latter months of the war the burden of home defence rested almost entirely on the shoulders of the naval air squadrons that had survived the slaughter in the Pacific.

By July 1945 huge formations of B-29s, joined now by fighter-bombers from the carrier task-forces that had battled their way across the Pacific, were roaming freely over the skies of Japan. With her aircraft industry in ruins, it was now that Japan keenly felt the effect of the massive losses suffered during the previous months – including the sacrifice of hundreds of aircraft and pilots in fruitless *kamikaze* suicide attacks. A plan to use almost every remaining aircraft in more suicide missions against the Allied invasion force that was assembling to invade Japan was forestalled by the dropping of the atomic bombs on Hiroshima and Nagasaki, and the Japanese surrender.

11 Jet Combat

The advent of the jet fighter in the skies of Europe during the closing stages of the Second World War brought about a dramatic change in the science of air combat; it was not, however, a sudden change, and when the next major conflict – the Korean War – broke out in June 1950, it was still the piston-engined fighter that formed the nucleus of the belligerents' bid for air supremacy.

The mainstay of the North Korean Air Force during the early stages of the Communist offensive across the 38th parallel was the Yak-9 fighter, the type that had helped to carry the Soviet Air Force to victory five years earlier. Other types in service with this Soviet-trained air arm were the Yak-3, the Lavochkin La-7 and the Ilyushin Il-10 Sturmovik. Opposing them were North American P-51 Mustangs and P-82 Twin Mustangs, together with smaller numbers of P-80 Shooting Stars – the USAF's first jet fighters.

These types quickly enabled the Americans to establish air superiority, and by the end of August the North Korean Air Force had been practically wiped out. Then, in October, Chinese Communist forces intervened on a massive scale, and United Nations pilots began to encounter a new enemy combat aircraft: the Russian-built MiG-15 jet fighter, a swept-wing, cannon-armed machine that was capable of a speed of 650 mph and was clearly far superior to anything the Americans had in Korea at that time.

The only American fighter that could match the MiG-15 in performance was the North American F-86A Sabre, and by the middle of December 1950 the first Sabre unit – the 4th Intercepter Wing – had been rushed into action in Korea. During preliminary skirmishes with the MiGs, it was found that the Sabre's biggest disadvantage was its limited radius of action; whereas the MiGs operated within sight of their own airfields, the Sabres had to make the long trip north to the Yalu River from their bases at Kimpo or Taegu, which reduced the time they could spend in the combat area to a matter of minutes. To extend their patrol time the Sabres were forced to fly at relatively low airspeeds to conserve fuel, which placed them at a distinct disadvantage. The MiG pilots were quick to exploit the Sabres' weakness, attacking from above at near-sonic speed and making their escape before the Sabre pilots could increase their own speed enough to react. To counter this the Sabre pilots adopted new tactics which involved sending four flights of F-86s into the combat area at five-minute intervals and at high speed; from then on, although the Communists almost always enjoyed the initial advantage, the Sabres began to establish definite air supremacy.

By June 1951 the Chinese Communists had over three-hundred MiG-15s concentrated on their airfields north of the Yalu – a formidable force against which the Americans had only forty-four Sabres in Korea. It was a considerable source of annoyance and frustration to the United Nations pilots that they were not allowed to cross the river to strike at the enemy on his bases. Nevertheless, despite the fact that they were often outnumbered by

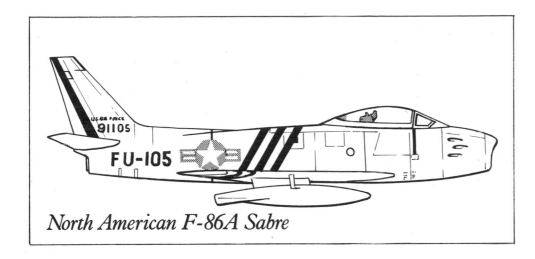

North American F-86A Sabre

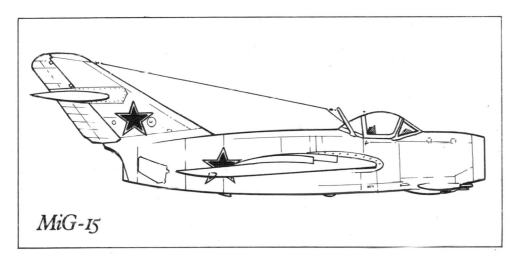

MiG-15

two to one in air combat, the Sabres managed to hold their own – although the MiGs challenged their overall superiority several times. It was touch and go in September and October 1951, when the MiGs succeeded for the first time in seriously interfering with American bombing raids on North Korean targets, and the situation only eased in January 1952, with the arrival in Korea of a second Sabre Wing: the 51st.

The United Nations retained its air supremacy throughout 1952, and a number of pilots in the ranks of the Sabre squadrons became the world's first jet fighter aces. The top-scorer was Captain Joseph McConnell of the 51st Wing, who shot down sixteen MiGs before the war ended in 1953; close behind him came Major James Jabara, who shot down 15 MiGs in two combat tours. In equal third place were Captain Manuel J. Fernandez and Lieutenant-Colonel George A. Davis, both of the 4th Wing, with 14 victories apiece; Davis was killed in action on 10 February 1952 while fighting against greatly superior odds; he was awarded a posthumous Congressional Medal of Honor.

As a Korean armistice became a possibility in the early summer of 1953, the last great jet-versus-jet battles of the conflict took place as Sabres and MiGs hurled themselves at one another in a series of frenzied dogfights. In June the United Nations claimed the destruction of 77 enemy fighters, with 11 probably destroyed and 41 damaged. No friendly aircraft was lost.

By the time the last shots of the Korean War were fired United Nations

LEFT Sea Furies on board
HMS *Glorious* rev up for action off
the coast of North Korea.

BELOW A North American F-86D
Sabre in flight.

OPPOSITE A MiG being shot down
over Hanoi in June 1967.

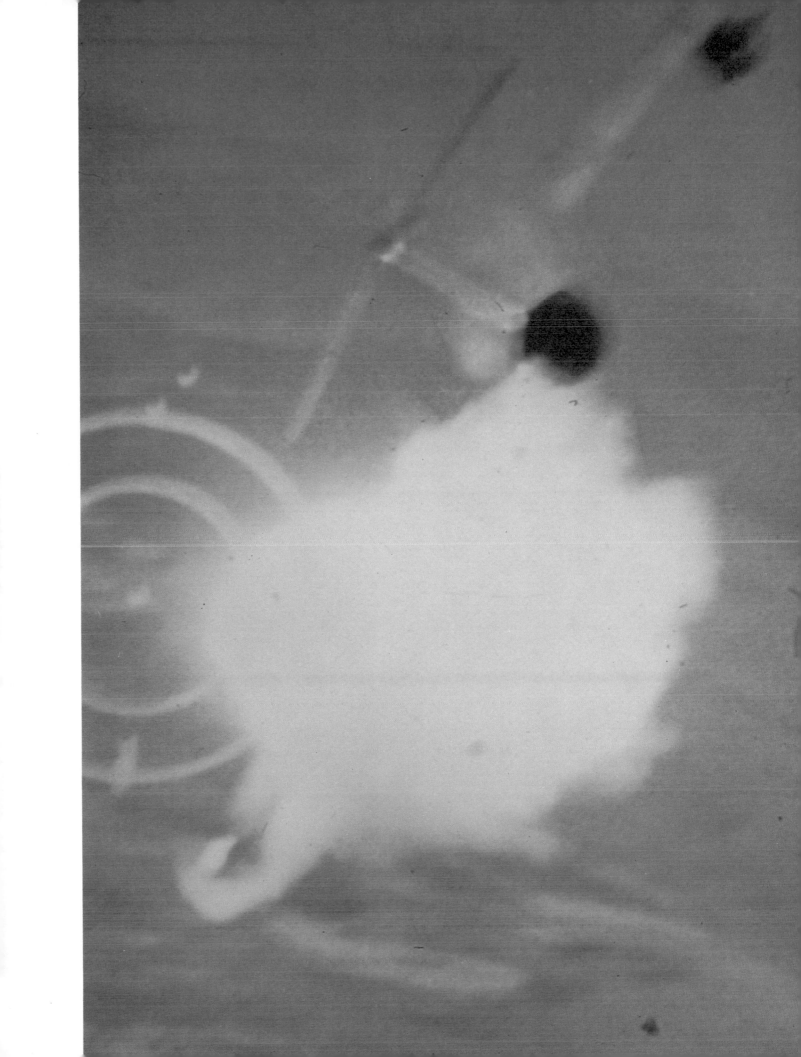

airmen claimed to have destroyed 900 enemy aircraft in three years of fighting, a total that included 792 MiG-15s claimed by the Sabre pilots for the loss of 78 of their own number. There is no reason to doubt these claims, for the great majority were recorded accurately on film. The reason for the Sabres' ten-to-one kill ratio over aircraft that were technically their match was a combination of many factors, not the least of which was the higher overall standard of training among United Nations pilots. Also, the Sabre was the better weapon system; a better combination of airframe, engine, guns and pilot. Its six 0.5-inch machine-guns proved to be more effective than the MiGs' heavy 23-mm and 37-mm cannon, which – although ideal for knocking down bombers – had a rate of fire that was too slow for air combat at near-sonic speeds.

In October 1956, a little over three years after the end of the Korean conflict, the jet fighters of East and West once again met in combat – this time over the Sinai Desert, where Egyptian MiG-15s battled with the French-built Dassault Ouragans and Mystères of the Israeli Air Force. During the Sinai Campaign the Mystère IVA showed itself to be a better aircraft than the MiG

TOP A MiG-17 caught by Israeli cannon fire on a Sinai airfield, 5 June 1967.

ABOVE A USAF B-52 Stratofortress unloads its bombs on enemy positions in South Vietnam.

RIGHT USAF F-105 Thunderchiefs in action over North Vietnam. The single lead aircraft is an A-3 Skywarrior providing radar guidance for the bombers.

on every count except rate of climb. Instead of using the latter to their advantage, Egyptian MiG pilots persisted in trying to out-turn the Israeli fighters, a manœuvre that often ended with the Russian-built machine flicking into a spin.

Ten years later Arab and Israeli fighters were once again locked in battle during the Six-Day War of 1967; on this occasion Israeli air superiority was assured right from the start by their massive pre-emptive strike on the Arabs' air-bases, and the Egyptian, Syrian and Jordanian fighters that managed to get off the ground were quickly overwhelmed. During these air battles Israeli pilots made an interesting observation: that in the heat of a dogfight cannon were much more effective in shooting down an adversary than the air-to-air missiles with which both sides were now armed. In Vietnam United States Air Force and Navy pilots, flying the latest F-105 Thunderchief, A-4 Skyhawk and F-4 Phantom fighter-bombers, came to the same conclusion; in the course of several air battles that took place during the bombing offensive against North Vietnam in 1966, when American fighters tangled with Russian-built MiG-17s and MiG-21s, it was usually

ABOVE A Hawker Siddeley Harrier
Mark I firing SNEB rockets
in flight.

RIGHT An F-4M Phantom II
fighter-bomber intercepting a
Tupolev Tu-95, Bear.

BELOW An F-4D Phantom II
armed with a modular guided
glide bomb.

cannon fire that decided the outcome. On one occasion a Phantom pilot fired all four of his Sidewinder missiles at a MiG-21 without scoring a single hit.

ABOVE The F-15 Eagle armed with Sparrow missiles.

In terms of modern air combat, the day of the pure intercepter fighter is over. Although manned strategic bombers such as Russia's new 'Backfire' and America's B-1 will be in evidence for years to come, and the ability to destroy them remain of vital importance, it is air superiority over the battlefield that is the decisive factor in any modern war. For this reason both the Americans and Russians are developing a new generation of 'air superiority' fighters: highly manœuvrable aircraft armed with a wide variety of weapons and capable of dogfighting at anything from a few hundred knots to more than twice the speed of sound.

The race to find the ideal fighter, begun by Anthony Fokker more than half a century ago, continues today unchecked: and the air-fighting formula of sun, height and speed, evolved over Flanders by the young men of a lost generation, holds good even in the jet age.

Further Reading

Bekker, Cajus. *The Luftwaffe War Diaries*. London, 1966; New York, 1975.

Bishop, Edward. *The Battle of Britain*. London, 1960.

Bishop, W. A. *Winged Warfare*. London.

Cole, C. *Royal Flying Corps 1915–1926*. London, 1969.

Fokker, Anthony and Gould, Bruce. *Flying Dutchman – the Life of Anthony Fokker*. London and New York, 1972.

Harvey, Frank, *Air War – Vietnam*. London, 1967.

Haughland, V. *The AAF against Japan*. New York, 1948.

Jackson, Robert, *The Red Falcons – Soviet Air Force in Action 1918–1969*. London and New York, 1970.

Jackson, Robert. *The Israeli Air Force Story*. London and New York, 1970.

Jackson, Robert. *Air War over Korea*. Shepperton, 1974; New York, 1975.

Jackson, Robert. *Air War over France, 1939–40*. Shepperton, 1975.

Jensen, O. *Carrier War*. New York, 1945.

Jones, H. A. *The War in the Air* (12 volumes). London.

Playfair, I. S. O. *The Mediterranean and Middle East* (4 volumes). London, 1960.

Sherrod, R. *History of Marine Corps Aviation in World War II*. Washington DC, 1952.

Shores, C. and Ring, Hans. *Fighters over the Desert*. London, 1969.

Wykeham, P. *Fighter Command*. London, 1960.

Acknowledgments

Photographs and illustrations are supplied by or reproduced by kind permission of the following:

Bapty & Co.: *58, 59, 62-3*; Baratt's Photo Press Ltd: 69 above; Bayer Armeemuseum, München: 50; Bibliothek f. Zeitgesch., Stuttgart: 31 left; Blitz Publications: *123 below*; Camera Press: 109, 111, 112, 118; Crown Copyright, Ministry of Defense (RAF): 154 above left and above right; Culver Pictures Inc.: 51 above; Daily Mail: 89; Flight International: 152 above; Fox Photos: 130 above; Fujiphotos: 136; K. M. Molson Collection: 24 above and below, 40 below; J. G. Moore Collection: *14*, 134-5, 138, 142, 143, 145, 146 below, *150 below*, 151, 152 below, 152-3, *154 below*, 155; Musee de l'Air: 25 above and below left; Novosti Press Agency: 110 above and below, 116; Planet News: 150 above; RAF/Robert Jackson: 100; RAF Staff College: *26-7, 38-9*; Roger-Viollet: 13, 15 below; Spitfire Productions Ltd: *66-7*/David James, *71*/David James, *73*/David James, *75 above*/David James, *75 below*/John Young, *79*/John Young, *81*/David James, *82*/David James, *86*/Keith Hamshcrc; Staatsbibliothek, Berlin: 17; Suddeutsche Verlag: 16 below, 43, 45, 52 above; Ullstein: 19 above left and right, 36, 52 below; USAF, Virginia: *150 below*, 151, 152 below, 152-3, *154 below*, *155*; US Navy/National Archives, Washington: 134-5, 135, 138, 142, 143, 145, 146 below; US War Department General Staff/National Archives: 49, 51 below.

Numbers in italics rcfcr to colour illustrations.

Maps and line drawings by D.P. Press.

Index